THE WAY OF LANGUAGE
AN INTRODUCTION

FRED WEST

HARCOURT BRACE JOVANOVICH, INC.

New York   Chicago   San Francisco   Atlanta

To my friend Dr. Emmett Cockrum,
without whose cheerful assistance
this book could not have been written.

ISBN: 0–15–595130–0

Library of Congress Catalog Card Number: 74–11793

Printed in the United States of America

CREDITS AND ACKNOWLEDGMENTS

Cartoon, page 15, copyright by John A. Ruge. Reproduced with permission of Saturday Review/World.

Table 4-3, page 80, from *Language* by Leonard Bloomfield. Copyright, 1933, by Holt, Rinehart and Winston, Inc. Copyright renewed © 1961, by Leonard Bloomfield. Adapted and reprinted by permission of Holt, Rinehart and Winston, Inc.

PREFACE

While practically all of us know how to use language, many of us know very little *about* language. This book is intended to introduce the reader, student and layman alike, to the nature of language—the elements that make up language, the effect that language has on the individual and on society, and the forces that cause language to change continually. In order to present as broad a picture as possible within the framework of an introductory book, *The Way of Language* takes a chronological approach: it begins with a discussion of what people in early times, including the Egyptians and the Greeks, thought about language, and ends with some observations about the future of language and language study, especially the use of electronic computers in linguistics. The chronological approach also serves to show the reader that much of our modern thinking about language is actually based on ideas of long ago.

The chapters on the structure of language—phonology, morphology, syntax, and grammar—are fairly traditional in approach. The book breaks with tradition in its wider use of non-Indo-European languages as examples and illustrations—Vietnamese, Eskimo, and Arabic, among others. Contemporary American languages and dialects, particularly Black English and the American Indian languages, are discussed in some detail. The diversity of illustrations is intended to emphasize the equality and integrity of all languages, no matter how they differ from one another. The chapters on structure are, of course, more technical than the others and contain a number of unfamiliar terms and concepts. The reward of seeing language from a new viewpoint, however, is worth the effort of learning those terms. Tables and illustrations are used extensively throughout the book to explain and clarify specific points, and a Glossary is provided to define useful terms.

Thanks are due to Professors Mark Molander, De Anza

College, Cupertino, California; George O'Neill, Savannah State College; and William Stacey, Colorado State University, for reading and criticizing the manuscript. I am particularly grateful to Professor Charlton Laird, of the University of Nevada at Reno, who not only read and criticized the manuscript of *The Way of Language*, but has encouraged me in my other works as well.

Fred West

CONTENTS

I

THE SPREAD
OF LANGUAGE

In the beginning was the Word, and the Word
was with God. . . .

John 1:1

I

INTRODUCTION:
THE ORIGIN OF LANGUAGE

People have always speculated upon how language began;
consequently, we have with us today an extensive collection of
theories and guesses, some rather ridiculous, others with more
than a trace of credibility to them. In 1866 the French Société
de Linguistique forbade any discussion at its meetings of the
origins of language, on the grounds that such speculation was
absolutely fruitless. Nevertheless, speculation continues. We
are still curious about how it all began.

Most recently certain feminists have pointed out that
language is a powerful brainwasher (which it is) and a prehistoric
device invented by men to perpetuate the myth of masculine
superiority. Just look at such vocabulary items as "man,"

"*man*kind," "hu*man*ity." And according to ancient, *man*-recorded Scriptures, the first human creation of God was a *man* named "Adam," which in Hebrew means "man."

Ancient Theories

Before the middle of the eighteenth century, theories of the beginning of language generally fell into the category of DIVINE ORIGIN. According to these early theories, man was created almost instantaneously, and at the moment of his creation speech was provided him as a divine gift. So goes the biblical story of the Garden of Eden. God created Adam and speech simultaneously, for God spoke with Adam and Adam answered him. The language they used was Hebrew.

However, there have been exceptions in the Judeo-Christian world to the believers in Hebrew as the original tongue. In the seventeenth century, Andreas Kemke, a Swedish philologist, patriotically asserted that in the Garden of Eden God spoke Swedish, Adam spoke Danish, and the serpent spoke French. One wonders what the French had done to offend the good Swede. Another patriotic theorist was the sixteenth-century Dutchman Goropius Becanus, who asserted that the language of the Garden was Dutch. It was probably from his statement that Elizabethan dramatist Ben Jonson borrowed the words: "I'll show you a treatise penned by Adam—and in High Dutch. Which proves it was the primitive tongue."

Of course, other cultures had divinely inspired original languages, too. The Egyptians considered themselves the oldest civilization; therefore, the original language was Egyptian, passed on to the humans of ancient Egypt through their god-ancestors. This assumption was checked out at least once, according to the historian Herodotus. A seventeenth-century B.C. Egyptian ruler named Psammetichus had enough curiosity to try an experiment. On the premise that babies, if left alone, will grow up speaking "the" original language, Psammetichus had two babies taken at random from an ordinary family and given to a shepherd to raise. He ordered the shepherd to speak not a word to the babies, only tend to their needs. When they were two years old, the little ones one day abruptly greeted the shepherd with "*Becos!*" The shepherd immediately reported this to Psammetichus, who checked it with his counselors. The counselors informed the king that *becos* meant "bread" in Phrygian, so in true scientific spirit Psammetichus announced that Phrygian was the original language.

Just as the first divinely descended Egyptian pharaoh brought speech to man, so did the Chinese emperor T'ien-tzu, the Son of Heaven. In Japan, the divine creator of man, complete with language, was Amaterasu, the sun goddess. In the Middle East it was Enlil, "the spirit of the word which stilleth the heaven above." The Greco-Roman chief god was Zeus-pater, or Jupiter, the "father of light." When we find practically the same myths about the creation of man and language occurring in American Indian folklore, we are irresistibly attracted by the psychologist Carl Jung's belief in a *collective unconscious*, a vast common reservoir collecting all of mankind's unconscious memories; from this reservoir rise similar patterns of experience and behavior among different peoples. These archetypal, or basic, forms reveal themselves in religion, art, and myth. Myth has been defined as the story preserved in popular memory of a past event, the original history of mankind. One recurring characteristic of the creation myths of the American Indians is the function of the light god. The creator-teacher of the Mayas was Itzamna, also known as Kin-ich-ahau, which translates into "Lord of the sun's face," or the dawn. The culture god of the Iroquois was Ioskeha, "about-to-grow-white," or, again, the dawn. The Algonquian deity was Michabo, god of light.

So we see that generally the creator-god was also a light god. We can interpret the myths, then, as saying that language came with the dawn of reason. And since LINGUISTICS, the scientific study of language, cannot be studied in a vacuum any more than can any other discipline, we must consider the findings and theories of such kindred subjects as psychology, anthropology, sociology, and poetry. If we accommodate our thinking to primitive expression as revealed through mythology, then we may suppose that at least subconsciously these so-called primitive peoples were not actually stating an instantaneous, or mechanistic, creation of language, but were more likely personifying the evolution of developing man to a point where language became a necessity.

The Greeks were more vague than mystic about the origin of language. Since the ancient Greeks gave the name *barbaros*—a word meaning "foreigner" and suggesting "babbler"—to all non-Greeks, it is easy to surmise that they felt that Greek comprised everything a language needs. Plato (c. 400 B.C.) in his *Cratylus* has his spokesman Socrates discuss language. This dialogue, sometimes called Plato's dullest, is actually fascinating —at least to the linguist—because it contains such a combination of nonsense and intelligent insights about language. Among the former is an obvious reason why Socrates didn't get along with his wife, Xanthippe. Insisting that men are wiser than women (his premise), Socrates cites the case of the naming of Hector's son in the *Iliad*. The women called the babe Scamandrius, after the name of a river, an insignificant appellation for the future hero. But the men of Troy called him Astyanax, which means "king of the city," a far more heroic and appropriate name. Therefore, the correct, or natural, names are given by the wise (the men).

Socrates argues throughout the dialogue that things have names *by nature*. All names, he says, were intended to indicate the nature of things; the ancients formed language by using the appropriate letters to fit appropriate concepts. For example, Greek ρ ("r") was used in words suggesting motion, such as *krovein* ("strike"), *thravein* ("crush"), *thryptein* ("break"), because in forming the letter ρ the tongue was most agitated. Socrates argues his point further, stating that natural names may have a letter or two misplaced and still be legitimate. For example, *eiros* ("hero") is derived from *eros* (Eros was the god of love) because heroes sprang either from the love of a god for a mortal woman, or of a mortal man for a goddess.

It's hard to tell if Socrates is being serious or simply joking.

Other speakers in the dialogue, however, come out with definitely serious insights, such as "the name is not the same with the thing named"—the argument that names are merely *conventional*. Plato's pupil Aristotle argued this view further in his essay *On Interpretation*: "All is convention and habit of users." Modern-language teachers know from experience that to break the bond between *words* and *things* in the native language is one of the hardest steps for a student in learning another language. To the American student, "bread" is *bread*. How can it be *pan*, as in Spanish, or *psomi*, as in Greek?

Later Theories

Speculation on the origin of language moved from the realm of fancy and entered what is called the "organic phase" in the latter part of the eighteenth century with the publication of Johann Gottfried von Herder's *Über den Ursprung der Sprache* (*On the Origin of Language*) in 1772. This was the period when Immanuel Kant and others set the stage for the theory of the evolution of man, so well stated about a century later by Charles Darwin. Herder argued that language was too imperfect to have been a divine gift; it came about through man's own groping efforts toward reasoning. Language, he said, was the result of an "instinctive impulse similar to that of an embryo pressing to be born."

Darwin argued against any distinctly "human" quality of language. In *Descent of Man* (1871), he maintained that there is only a difference of degree between the language of man and the cries of animals. He reasoned that man's language, like man himself, came from a more primitive form, probably expressions of emotion. For example, the feeling of contempt or disgust is accompanied by a tendency to puff out air through the nose or mouth, and this makes such sounds as "Pooh!" or "Pish!" Max Müller, a contemporary who disagreed with Darwin on this point, nicknamed it scornfully the POOH-POOH theory.

Darwin's argument was pretty well discredited by later

scholars such as Edward Sapir, who pointed out that language is directed toward someone to achieve a result. An involuntary cry of pain can come with no intent to communicate. This counterargument works well enough as far as separating speech from animal cries, but who can say what actually went on at the dawn of reason? At some time in his development, primitive man learned to classify and manipulate sounds for a purpose, but the sounds had to come first.

In the twentieth century Edgar Sturtevant humorously proposed that language developed from emotive expressions for the purpose of lying. That is, originally the cries and other expressions of fear, pain, and anger were involuntary utterances. Then, when a man—a very perceptive primitive man—noticed the submissiveness of his mate when he roared with anger, he deliberately developed the involuntary sound-symbol as a tool to keep his domestic affairs under control. He faked anger when he actually felt none, thus becoming the proto-liar.

Müller, the greatest popularizer of linguistics in the nineteenth century, proposed what he called the DING-DONG theory of the origin of language. Somewhat similar to Socrates' argument that language came about naturally, Müller's theory claimed a mystic harmony or correlation between sound and meaning. In primitive man was an instinct by which every impression from without received its vocal expression from within. Just as in nature every object, when struck by a solid body, gave off its own peculiar sound (like a bell when it is struck), so man's mind gave off a particular response to the various impacts which the world made upon it. There were four hundred or so basic sounds which made up the roots of this original language. For example, when primitive man was confronted by a wolf, the sight rang a bell, so to speak, and he instinctively said, "Wolf!" Müller later rejected his own theory.

Another theory which we can mention briefly is the YO-HE-HO theory. This theory suggests that language first began in a social setting (which is valid enough so far), that of men working together. Strong muscular action, such as a man swinging an axe or a sledgehammer, caused the breath to be expelled forcibly for relief. The vocal cords vibrated, a specific rate of vibration for a specific action, thus producing a particular and distinct sound for each particular kind of work. The sound identified with that action became the name of the action: "Heave!" "Haul!" "Push!" Grunts do indeed result from muscular exertions, and some of these grunts may become incorporated in words or word formations. But to assume an entire language built from grunts is rather ridiculous.

A more tenacious theory has been the BOW-WOW theory, so named by the energetic Max Müller. Also referred to as ONOMATOPOETIC or ECHOIC, the theory suggests that first words were imitative of natural sounds: the cry of birds, the call of animals, the noise of storms, rivers, and so on. Müller rejected this theory, commenting sarcastically that it applied very well to cackling hens and quacking ducks, but the bulk of language operates outside the barnyard.

However, no matter how small the percentage, virtually every known language has some echoic words in its vocabulary, mainly nouns and verbs. In English we have "babble," "rattle," "hiss," "ripple," "pee-wee," "cuckoo," "hiccup." The dictionary lists scores of others as imitative, and they keep coming in. "Burp" has now been extended to "burp gun"; "zip" developed into both verb and noun, and extended to "zipper." Earlier forms of English may reveal this echoic quality more than their modern forms. For example, "laugh," which doesn't necessarily sound echoic today, derives from Old English *hlæhhan* or *hliehhan*. Keeping in mind that in Old English initial *h*'s were strongly aspirated, or huffed, pronounce these words and note the obvious imitation of a laugh. We also have "slurp," which is quite similar to its Dutch original, *slurpen*, a sound-symbol recognizable to all enjoyers of soup. The English signal for silence "Sshh!" isn't too far from Latin *susurrus*, meaning "whisper."

An argument against the onomatopoetic theory of the origin of language is that we hear and imitate the sounds of nature *within the limitations of our first language*. That means, of course, the language of the culture we are raised in, not the so-called original language. Textbooks frequently cite as an example of cultural influence the fact that a rooster crowing in English says "Cock-a-doodle-doo"; in French, "*Coquerico*"; in Italian, "*Chiccirichi*"; in German, "*Kikeriki*." This example really proves nothing, however, because all these languages stem from the same PROTO-LANGUAGE (or "ancestor" language) and are daughter languages in the same linguistic family. A case could possibly be made that in the proto-language these sounds were one. A better argument to support the "limitations of our first language" would be to bring in terms that are not from our own language family. For example, the echoic word for "thunder" is, in French, *tonnere*; in German, *Donner*; but in Keresan (an American Indian language group), *ko-o-muts*.

An interesting fact that has surfaced as a result of studies in languages of primitive cultures is that some of the most primitive cultures use the least number of echoic speech items, while a sophisticated language like English with its half-a-million word-hoard uses perhaps the most. And apparently this characteristic of English existed even before the language was first recorded.

Even more hardy than the bow-wow theory is the GESTURE theory, which states that words and language developed from meaningful gestures. According to Darwin, while the hands were employed in gestural signals, they could not be used for other necessary work. Nor could hand signals be transmitted and received in the dark. Something else was needed: vocal signals were inevitable. Around the turn of the twentieth century, Wilhelm Wundt, an experimental psychologist, elaborated considerably on this theory, and reputable linguists and psychologists continue to discuss it. Certainly if we accept the premise that language did not suddenly emerge fully developed one bright day, then it follows that language evolved out of some proto-communication system. Most likely that system was vocal gesture, such as anthropoid apes use. Then, at some intermediate stage during the millennia of trial and error, progress—or even survival—depended more upon vocalization and less on gesture. Perhaps, as Darwin suggested, because it was dark, or he had his hands full, or his companion was not looking, primitive man had to communicate, so he gestured with his tongue, simultaneously making a sound. If we think of speech as a form of activity, as vocal behavior, then it is comparable to movements of legs and arms.

It is also reasonable to think that vocal language came after gesture because man actually has no separate physical equipment for speech. (However, a current view is that the speech organs are too finely adjusted for the specific purpose of speech to have evolved simply for nourishment and breathing.) Speech is formed in the passage which is used primarily for eating and breathing. The nose is primarily for respiration. The tongue aids in eating. All these parts and others are used in creating speech, not uniformly but arbitrarily according to different languages. The French, like certain Pueblo Indians, have many nasalized sounds, thus using the nose more than, say, the British do. The Spanish make great use of the tip of the tongue, while the Arabs use the back of the tongue and the throat muscles a great deal. Some cultures make more use of the lips than do others—like the Hottentots, who use a kissing movement to produce smacks that constitute sound-meaning in their language. The Hottentots also use a sharp intake of air to make clicks which shape meaning for them. Sinitic languages include tones: *yu* in Mandarin, the Peking dialect of Chinese, can mean ''fish,'' ''mud,'' ''gem,'' ''feather,'' or become a prepositional particle, all depending upon whether the tone is rising, high level, dipping, or dropping abruptly.

Modern Theories

The physical equipment was there for the production of speech. But speech is not simply a manipulation of physical limbs and organs. Psychological development was needed, too. Speech, as language, is the result of man's ability to see phenomena symbolically and of the necessity to express his symbols. For example, a man looking at a natural phenomenon like a river sees not just a flowing body of water; to him, the river may symbolize a destructive agent which could drown him. To another man the river might symbolize just the opposite; he might see a supply of life-giving liquid for plants and animals. Another man might see the river as an environment for fish. Still another might see it as a cool, comfortable place to swim on a hot day. To communicate these different psychological impressions, man needed more word-symbols, such as "cool," "wet," "dangerous," "good," and so on. In order for us to come up with a credible theory of the origin of language, we will have to know a great deal more about the psychological development of early man.

Most anthropologists today agree that man as we know him and language developed together. This does not mean that the appearance of either was instantaneous. According to the geological time scale, man came into existence during the Pleistocene Epoch, which means he has been on earth for a million years or more. The factors which led to the development of *Homo sapiens* also led to the development of language. Man's posture became upright, giving him additional visual range; his eyes became stereoscopic, further improving his vision by increasing his three-dimensional depth perception. The cerebral cortex, virtually nonexistent in fish and other lower creatures, developed tremendously in evolving man. With this development of his brain, he passed from subhuman to human. He graduated from a sort of trial-and-error learning to reasoning powers; he began to invent and use tools; and he began to speak.

Just as the developing human embryo appears to represent the developing stages of man from the primordial fishlike creature to the perfectly formed human, so, some believe, the development of language is re-enacted in the child. A highly respected linguist of the early part of the twentieth century, Otto Jespersen, saw the pattern of babies' sounds in the prelearning stage as representative of human language at the dawn of man. He believed that man's first "language" was near-meaningless, but musical, very much like the crooning and singing of a baby. Then, with additional power and flexibility, he added to this birdlike singing sounds like the roaring of animals and various exclamations, although he was not yet truly communicating ideas.

However that may be, our new man certainly became a social creature. Language evolved from the need of humans to signal to each other and from their developing mental capacity to accommodate symbolism and construct a system of word-symbols. It might seem that at this point we are confronted with the old dilemma of which came first, the chicken or the egg. In other words, if our early men were not living in society, they would not need language, but how could they live in society without language? Dilemma or not, the fact remains that we have both the chicken and the egg, language and society.

The same development which enabled man to construct a language also enabled him to construct tools. The use of tools is largely a cooperative enterprise, dependent upon the coordination of the activities of individuals. For our primitive toolmakers to coordinate the intelligent behavior involved in the use of tools, language was necessary. So language developed in a social situation and functioned to spread information throughout a group. It enabled one person to take advantage of the experiences of several other persons. Each gained in power: a hunter, a fisherman, an axe-maker, a boat-builder, all contributed to each member of a social group. Language became man's principal device for welding together a group for cooperative action. Subsequently, the whole working of human society, through a division of labor, has been due to language.

Obviously, tools, language, and society didn't come into being so suddenly. Prolific and profligate Nature must have wasted a myriad humanoids over thousands of years before the right combination caught on. Inefficient types died out, killed off in war or by savage animals, possibly because they were unable to speak or understand basic signals like "Duck!" or "Over here, you idiot!"

To compress the whole symbolic process into a single time-and-space setting, we might imagine a little scenario of about 1,000,000 B.C. Ik, Ak, and Ok are planning the mammoth kill. They need meat for the tribe, and they know the trail by which the huge animals come to the upper meadow to graze. The trail goes through a pass about fifty yards in width; on one side rises a sheer cliff; on the other side is a steep drop of several hundred feet. Ak is all for following the procedure of the previous year: hide among the small boulders at either end of the pass, and when several of the mammoths are in the pass, the entire tribe will rush in with flaming torches and drive the creatures over the edge to their death. Voilà! Food!

But Ik has been fiddling around for several days with a new device. In an axe-wielding battle with a large wolf some months before, he had gotten nipped pretty badly in the thigh before finishing off the sharp-fanged predator. While recovering from his wound, he had speculated long and hard on how to kill without close contact. The idea finally came to him when he saw his little son throwing sticks at a bird. Why not attach a pointed stone, slimmer and sharper than an axehead, to a long stick and throw it?

Now he proposes arming all the men of the tribe with spears, blockading the mammoths as before, but instead of running them over the drop, the men would pen them against the opposite cliff and kill them with spears.

"Why?" asks Ak.

"Because," reasons Ik, "they won't get so smashed up, and we won't have to haul all that heavy stuff back up from way down there."

Ok, who is a trifle lazy, agrees.

So by recalling the past and planning for the future, man advanced to time-binding. His mind broke through the sense-limiting medium of time and he was now able to hold the continuum of time—present, past, and future—simultaneously in his mind through word-symbols. To expand his new world of objects, events, space, time, and qualities such as mass, velocity, form, color, texture, he created yet more word-symbols. With more ideas to think about and discuss with his companions, he increased his inventory of word-symbols, originally indicators of concrete phenomena that he could see close at hand, to include more abstract symbols. With these new words he communicated to others the unseen danger of the distant river and of the great cave bear. Such words in turn allowed even more abstractions of thought. Society became more complex, and so did language. Thus cause became effect and effect became cause.

But again, we have no definite historical evidence to actually show the progression from a primitive language to a sophisticated one. As far back as we can trace languages historically, or even

"If I had my life to live over, I'd like to be born at anytime except the dawn of civilization!"

reconstruct them through the comparative method (which will be discussed later), they have all included words for such abstract concepts as bravery, nobility, deception, and freedom. This is equally true of the so-called primitive cultures today: they all have highly developed languages.

Is there really any good reason, then, to continue the search for an original theory? Some scholars think so. They feel that some tentative yet probable theory of its genesis is necessary to the development of an adequate psychology of language. But perhaps it's the other way around. According to psycholinguist Roger Brown, when we learn more about the psychology of language, we will be able to construct a satisfactory origin myth. At any rate, the study of language has always intrigued mankind, as the history of linguistics will show.

FOR FURTHER READING

"Brain," *Encyclopaedia Britannica.*

Burgess, Anthony, *Language Made Plain.* New York: Thomas Y. Crowell, 1965.

Gallant, Roy A., *Man Must Speak.* New York: Random House, 1969.

Jespersen, Otto, *Language.* New York: W. W. Norton, 1964.

Laird, Charlton, *The Miracle of Language.* New York: Fawcett World Library, 1972.

Paget, Richard, *Human Speech.* New York: Harcourt Brace Jovanovich, 1930.

Pei, Mario, *The Story of Language.* New York: New American Library, 1960.

Revesz, G., *The Origins and Prehistory of Language.* New York: Philosophical Library, 1956.

Schlauch, Margaret, *The Gift of Language.* New York: Dover, 1955.

Swadesh, Morris, *The Origin and Diversification of Language.* Chicago: Aldine Atherton, 1971.

There is no new thing under the sun. . . . Of
making of books there is no end.

Ecclesiastes 1:9, 12:12

The dominant philosophical system of each age
makes its imprint on each step in the evolution of
linguistic science.

Wade Baskin

2

A BRIEF HISTORY
OF LINGUISTICS

In order to give as broad a scope as possible to the subject
of this chapter, no matter how brief the treatment, we will
repeat the very general working definition of linguistics given in
Chapter 1 :

LINGUISTICS is the scientific study of language and languages.

The scientific study of language, as we interpret it today,
did not actually begin until the nineteenth century, and then it
was called not linguistics but comparative philology. Before that
came grammar and before that, rhetoric. We can begin with
RHETORIC, the use of language as a means of effective communication and persuasion.

The Earliest Linguists

The early Greeks, who originated, or at least thought of, practically everything, are said to have developed oratory in order to become persuasive lawyers, arguing about land titles. As a result, schools of rhetoric sprang up, and persuasive speech fell into organized patterns. That is, figures of speech and word-order arrangements became classified and standardized. Gorgias, a contemporary of Socrates, was one of the most outstanding of these early rhetoricians. He developed and gave names to various figures of speech still current today, such as antithesis, assonance, and puns. Of course, only the Greek language was used in these schools. We have already noted the chauvinistic attitude of the early Greeks toward their language, their belief that it contained all the essentials of language and that all other languages were inferior to it. Interestingly enough, the Greeks also believed that although words of different languages were different in form, the feelings behind these words were the same for all mankind. Similarly, our most modern and scientifically minded linguists concern themselves with the "universals" of language.

We have already discussed the origin of language according to Plato (*Cratylus*); now we must credit Plato with being one of the first grammarians. Just like modern grammarians, he proceeded first to divide the sentence into two parts, actor and action. His pupil Aristotle carried on from Plato's beginning, breaking up utterances into smaller components and classifying certain parts of speech. Aristotle also concerned himself with rhetoric and with PHONOLOGY, the study of the sound-units of speech. As a result of his writings on the subject, mainly *Rhetoric* and *Categories*, Aristotle has been called by some the "father of grammar in the Western world." (This question of paternity recurs all through the history of linguistics.)

About a hundred years later the Stoics, better known for their poker-faced resistance to emotion, attempted to separate grammar from philosophy. They improved somewhat on Aristotle's definitions and added still more to the general fund of knowledge about Greek grammar. They recognized and named the cases, tense, mood, voice, and other grammatical categories. They also introduced ETYMOLOGY (Greek *etyma* = ''roots''), the study of the origin and historical development of a word.

The high point of Greek linguistics came with the Alexandrian school, founded by Alexander the Great at Alexandria, then the capital of Egypt. The famous library of this school started from the personal library of Aristotle, teacher of Alexander. The prize linguistic product of the school was the *Grammar* of Dionysios Thrax (c. 100 B.C.). This little work of a few hundred lines became one of the most influential books in the world. It continued to be used in schools right up to the last century. Its familiarity will become obvious from its definition of the sentence: ''A sentence is a combination of words . . . making complete sense.'' The author named and defined eight parts of speech: noun, verb, participle, article, pronoun, preposition, adverb, and conjunction. He also attempted to distinguish phonologically between vowels and consonants.

To their great credit, the Greeks recognized language as a form of human behavior, and as such they attempted to systematize it.

At the same time that the Greeks, notably Plato and Aristotle, were toiling over linguistics, a Hindu grammarian named Panini (c. 400 B.C.) wrote what American linguist Leonard Bloomfield called one of the greatest monuments of human intelligence. For centuries Hindu priests, aware of the changing nature of language, had worked hard at preserving the ancient pronunciation and interpretation of the Brahmin sacred texts, one of which, the *Rig-Veda*, dates back at least to 1200 B.C. They felt that the holiness of the texts would diminish with the change from the original language forms, particularly in the pronunciation. Panini's grammar is the first known complete description of the structure of a language. While Panini's work was important in its own time—becoming the model for learned Sanskrit speakers, just as classical Latin remained the learned language for Europe for nearly two thousand years—it became even more important in the eighteenth and nineteenth centuries, when it was brought to the attention of European scholars, who were for the first time exposed to a complete and accurate description of a language.

At this point it would be well to recall that our ancestral linguists did not call themselves that name; probably they did not even think of themselves as linguists in the sense that we consider linguists today. They were philologists. The ancient Greeks called the various aspects of their study *philologos* and *grammatikos*. *Philologos* means "love of words," but the term philology has remained somewhat ambiguous right up to the present day. One of the definitions of philology has to do with classical scholarship. To the ancient Greeks that meant mainly the editing and interpretation of Homer; for the Hindu pandits it involved the preservation of the original forms of their sacred texts and hymns.

Since the study of language was influenced for such a very long time by Latin, we must take a look at some Latin contributions. Around the time of Julius Caesar, all educated Romans were well schooled in Greek, learned mainly from slave-tutors. The Romans had a great admiration of things Greek, and this extended to Greek grammar. Some Romans even considered Latin to be a daughter language of Greek. Marcus Terentius Varro (c. 75 B.C.), a learned Roman of his time, made a wholesale application of Greek grammar to Latin and came up with *De Lingua Latina*, a work that influenced all subsequent Latin grammarians. One astute contribution to linguistics by Varro was the flexible classification of words according to form or to their particular use in a given sentence, rather than an unvarying classification according to their meaning. This was a step repeated by Charles C. Fries in the twentieth century. Unfortunately, the almost blind worship of Greek caused later Latin grammarians to go back to Aristotle's system rather than to the more functional one of Varro.

Although the Stoics had started the study of etymology centuries earlier, it hadn't made much headway by the beginning of the Christian era. Quintilian, a famed rhetorician of the first century A.D., spent more time in speculation than he did in real linguistic research. (Early Greek and Roman intellectuals were more of the think-tank type than of the laboratory type.) For example, he reasoned "from contraries" that the Latin word *lucus*, meaning "a grove," must have derived from *lucendo*, "shining," because there is no light in a dense grove. This gem reappeared six hundred years later, as we will see.

Aelius Donatus, a Latin grammarian of the fourth century A.D., summed up what was then known about Latin grammar in his work *Ars Minor*. In philological tradition, he designed his work primarily for the analysis of classical writings, especially those of Virgil. Perhaps that is why Dante consigned Donatus to a particular place in hell in *The Divine Comedy*. Or perhaps the great medieval poet was simply rebelling in typical schoolboy fashion against a grammarian whose textbook was required study throughout the Middle Ages.

Donatus' book was the required elementary text; the more advanced text which served as authority for Latin scholars during the Middle Ages was the *Grammatical Categories* of Priscian (c. A.D. 550). Priscian's description of Latin grammar was the best available. Like grammarians today, he used as models for analysis actual quotations which he collected from speeches of educated orators. His work was adapted around A.D. 1000 by the eminent English scholar Aelfric into a textbook to teach Latin to English priests. Known today as Aelfric's *Colloquy*, its Latin has an interlinear gloss in lively, colloquial Anglo-Saxon. Bilingual education has been around for quite a while.

Linguistics in the Middle Ages and the Renaissance

One ill effect arising from such awed respect for early grammars and grammarians was the belief that the structure of languages, and particularly of classical Latin, is logical. There was some scattered rebellion against this attitude during the period now referred to as the twelfth-century Renaissance, but in general the traditional grammars were seldom challenged. In one form or another, however, the dispute continued that had begun in Plato's *Cratylus* over whether language has a natural logical quality or whether it is only a convention, an invented tool.

The questionable progress of the study of language through the Middle Ages may be demonstrated by a couple of excerpts from the *Etymologies* of Isidore of Seville (c. A.D. 600), a work quoted as authority for many centuries:

> The etymology of words is assigned from origin, like *homo* [Latin for "man"] from *humo* [Latin for "ground"].

> It is suspected that the Britons are so-called in Latin because they are brutes [Britones = *bruti*].

Isidore also included in his work the ridiculous "derivation by contraries" item by Quintilian, already cited.

This allegorical, even mystical, approach to etymology continued to be exploited with the introduction of Christianity into England, and persisted all through the Middle Ages. Pope Gregory (c. 575), according to the Venerable Bede's story, saw some young blond captives from Britain on the slave block in Rome. He asked what they were named. "Angles," was the reply. Said he, "Well that may be, for they have angelic faces." Then he asked what tribe they were from. His companions told him the captives had been taken from Deira. Said he, "Well, that is to say, *de ira eruti* ["from anger torn away"]; they shall be from God's anger rescued and to Christ's mercy made known." Then he asked who their king was, and when someone told him "Alle," he replied, "Alleluia! It befits that praise of God, our Creator, be sung in those parts." And soon afterwards he saw to it that some missionaries were sent to Britain.

One of the linguistic benefits resulting from the prose-lytizing zeal of missionaries, beginning with Saint Paul, has been the learning of other languages. In the fourth century the Scriptures were translated into Gothic; in the fifth, Armenian; and in the ninth, Old Church Slavonic. Translations of parts of sermons and scriptural passages paraphrased into local vernaculars to aid priests have given us our earliest records of certain languages, some of which are now extinct. In the twentieth century, the work of missionary-linguists all over the world has contributed immeasurably to the advancement of the scientific study of language. Much of the work in American Indian languages is being carried on at the present time by linguists of the Wycliffe Bible Translators.

The cause of linguistics in the Western world was greatly advanced by the Renaissance, largely through a radically increased awareness of other languages and other cultures. Beginning with the Platonic Academy in Florence and the reintroduction of Greek and Latin classics after the so-called Dark Ages, then the invention of the printing press by Johann Gutenberg in the middle of the fifteenth century, the Renaissance crested with the great wave of exploration set into motion by Columbus' discovery of the New World. Commerce flourished, and with it the need to communicate in other languages. By 1500, grammar books of most of the European languages were in print. By 1600, the list included grammars and word lists of Welsh, Basque, and other less-recognized languages. Also studied was Sanskrit, which was later to be so important to linguists.

Courtiers and diplomats of the Renaissance were also scholars, and when they had occasion to travel to other countries they wrote out phrase books of the languages they encountered. Some of these books have proved to be quite valuable today. The goal then was to transcribe all the known languages or at least to make word lists of them. In 1592 was published Hieronymus Megiser's *Specimens of Forty Languages*. Such philological activity went on until the beginning of the nineteenth century, when a work dealing with over eight hundred languages was written by Lorenzo Hervas y Panduro, undoubtedly the all-time record.

The Renaissance was also a period of linguistic chauvinism,

such as that demonstrated by the Dutchman Becanus and the Swede Kemke (see Chapter 1). King James IV of Scotland was a bit more religious than chauvinistic. Like Psammetichus of ancient Egypt, he is said to have performed the classic experiment with two tiny children to determine the original language. According to the traditional story, James reported that the children spoke Hebrew—not Scots.

For all its exuberant interest in just about everything, the Renaissance was still pretty much bound by medieval attitudes toward language, and particularly grammar. Scholars gathered a formidable amount of information about language, but they lacked the techniques of scientific analysis to do anything with this body of information. No real linguistic breakthrough occurred. The origin of the dialogue-type of language textbook for learning other languages, often in bilingual text, has been mistakenly attributed to the Renaissance period. Actually, Aelfric's *Colloquy*, written half-a-thousand years earlier, is of this type. Latin, Greek, and Hebrew remained the three sacred languages. Even in colonial America, the rakish scholar-statesman William Byrd read in one of these three languages nearly every morning before breakfast.

Of course, a few sporadic complaints against traditionalism arose from time to time: Montaigne the Frenchman, Locke the Englishman, and Leibniz the German, among others, commented upon education in general and language in particular. Leibniz, actually a post-Renaissance figure, is credited by many as being the first of the COMPARATIVE LINGUISTS, who study languages by noting the similarities and differences among them. Around the end of the seventeenth century this universal genius wrote a thesis proposing that broad groups of languages derived from a common ancestor, a proto-language, thus anticipating Sir William Jones by nearly a century. Leibniz interested himself enough in Russian to urge Czar Peter the Great to have dictionaries and grammars made of the many Russian languages, and, boldest of all, he published several of his own scholarly works in his native German rather than in academic Latin.

The Insistence on a "Pure" Language

After the Renaissance came the Age of Reason and a period of prescriptive grammar which, as we will see, had an ill effect and a good effect. The same mentality that had subscribed to the Great Chain of Being—that is, the belief that in the world-system there is an ordered place for everything—now advanced the idea that there was a "right" and a "wrong" grammar and that there were rules governing the correct form. Not only that; contemporary scholars saw in classical Latin the logical form of human speech. Italy, the birthplace of the Renaissance, had already led off with the Accademia della Crusca in 1546, a state-supported academy founded for the purpose of "purifying" and "fixing" the Italian language. At first, under pressure from the royal court, the literary people followed the rules laid down by the academy; then, through a combination of education and a desire to conform, most of the other people aspired to use the proper grammar and vocabulary.

Following the example of Italy, Cardinal Richelieu founded the prestigious Académie Française in 1635, with essentially the same methods and the same results. In 1660, Jansenist philologists at the Convent of Port-Royal, near Paris, produced the *Grammaire Générale et Raisonée*, a work which attempted to demonstrate that the structure of languages, particularly Latin, represents universally valid rules of logic. Next came Spain, in 1713, with the Real Academia Española.

Around the turn of the eighteenth century, Daniel Defoe and Jonathan Swift proposed that England follow the examples of Italy and France in establishing an academy to purify and "ascertain" the language. Fortunately, the freewheeling spirit of Shakespeare lived on. Most writers adjusted their style so they would be understood by the man in the street. No English academy was established. As to "fixing" the language in a permanent grammatical form, Richard Mulcaster, the teacher of the poet Edmund Spenser, had recognized, more than a hundred years earlier, that a language will inevitably change. Said he:

> When the age of our peple, which now use the tung so well, is dead and departed there will another succede, and with the people the tung will alter and change.

And at least two late-eighteenth-century grammarians, Joseph Priestly and George Campbell, expressed the view that usage, and not artificially derived rules, should determine the correctness of language. Campbell said that it is not the function of grammarians to give law, but to observe usage and to "note, collect, and methodise" it. What could be more modern?

The desire for a "pure" language did not originate with the movement in Western Europe. Much earlier, around A.D. 610, began the series of revelations to Mohammed, the Arabian prophet, that eventually was collected as the Koran, the holy book of the Muslims. Since much of the text is supposed to consist of the very words of Allah speaking to his prophet, and since Allah is perfection, then the language of the Koran must be perfection. On this premise, Al-Zabidi, an Iraqi scholar of the eleventh century, wrote *Lahn al-Awam*, a rulebook showing the mistakes of colloquial-Arabic speakers and the correct form from the Koran.

In style, diction, grammar, the Koran has remained the standard of Arabic for over thirteen centuries. A few years ago, when I worked in Saudi Arabia teaching English as a second language, if it became necessary to question my students about any points of grammar in Arabic, the students would go to the *cadi*, the religious magistrate, and get his opinion on the correct grammatical form. The *cadi*'s judgment was inevitably based on a perusal of the holy book, and his was the final word.

China, too, had her problems in language and literature, arising from a worship of the classical period of literature. As virtually all civilizations do, the Chinese harked back to a Golden Age when peace and goodness ruled the earth or, at least, ruled that particular culture. China's classics, supposedly dating from 2000 B.C., include *I-Ching*, *Odes* (poems in rhyme, a feature which does not appear in Latin poetry until a thousand *3000* years later), the *Analects* of Confucius, and other works. An academy of letters, the Hanlin, was founded in A.D. 754 and functioned right up to the nineteenth century. This academy is said to have been the example for those of Europe already mentioned. However, the literary purists of China fared no better than did those of England. Like classical Latin in the Western world, classical Chinese continued for centuries, but right along with it flourished drama, short stories, and novels in vernacular language.

A somewhat different situation occurred during the Heian period of Japan, which is considered the era of elegance and culture of that country. Chinese was for a long time the official language of the Japanese court; all members of court were supposed to be fluent in the language and in its poetry. (Ironically, one of the Chinese poets so frequently quoted by Japanese courtiers, Po Chu-i, had measured the success of his poems by how well they were understood and appreciated by the Chinese peasants, not the aristocrats.) All male members of court, that is—women didn't count. So it fell to the women to write in the lesser-regarded native Japanese language, and at least two of them produced world classics: Sei Shonagon's *Pillow-Book* and Lady Murasaki's *Tale of Genji* (both c. A.D. 1000). Soon after the end of the Heian era, Japanese became the accepted language of literature, although today scholars in Japan, as well as in Korea and Vietnam, are still able to read Chinese.

The Beginnings
of Modern Linguistics

A real movement toward scientific linguistic studies did not get underway until about the time of the American Revolution. Comparative philology—as contrasted with classical philology, which is not concerned with language per se—had its origin in the discovery that languages can be compared with one another. While this was a breathtaking discovery to linguists—or philologists—it didn't come with the suddenness of, say, a flight to the moon. A knowledge of Sanskrit—the event that started it all—had already come to Europe by way of missionaries by the sixteenth century. And at least one observant merchant of that century, an Italian named Filippo Sassetti, while in India noted the similarities between certain Italian words and corresponding words in Sanskrit:

	Italian	Sanskrit
god	*dio*	*deva*
snake	*serpe*	*sarpa*
seven	*sette*	*sapta*
eight	*otto*	*astau*
nine	*nove*	*nava*

Undoubtedly there were many others, scholars and nonscholars, who also drew conclusions about the similarities of Sanskrit to other European languages.

But the conclusions were limited. It remained for Sir William Jones to trigger the real breakthrough. Jones was a British civil servant, a judge in Calcutta. He was also a student of languages, including Sanskrit, and the founder of the Bengal Asiatic Society. It was to this society that he read his momentous paper in 1786. The key paragraph follows:

> The Sanskrit language, whatever be its antiquity, is of a wonderful structure; more perfect than the Greek, more copious than the Latin, and more exquisitely refined than either, yet bearing to both of them a stronger affinity, both in the roots of verbs and in the forms of grammar, than could possibly have been produced by accident; so strong indeed, that no philologer could examine them all three, without believing them to have sprung from some common source, which, perhaps, no longer exists: there is a similar reason, though not quite so forcible, for supposing that both the Gothic and the Celtic, though blended with a very different idiom, had the same origin with the Sanskrit; and the Old Persian might be added to the same family.

Soon after Jones' trailblazing statement, a number of "philologers," mainly German and Scandinavian, vied for the honored title of "father of comparative linguistics." In 1808 Friedrich von Schlegel published *Über die Sprache und Weisheit der Indier* (*On the Language and Wisdom of the Indians*), a work in which he discussed the relationship between German and Sanskrit. Of importance to the developing science of linguistics was Schlegel's introduction of the term "comparative grammar," the study of which he cited as one of the aims of scientific investigations of language. He also foreshadowed the Germanic consonantal sound-shift, which only a few years later was analyzed systematically by Grimm.

Rask, Bopp, and Grimm may be considered the "Big Three" of the nineteenth century. A polyglot as well as a linguist, the Dane Rasmus Rask began writing grammars of different languages almost from boyhood. In 1814 he wrote a prize-winning essay on the origin of Old Norse, in which he developed more fully the hint thrown out by Schlegel of the distinct kinship among the "Thracian" (INDO-EUROPEAN) languages.[1] Rask's method was to analyze several Scandinavian languages by applying the "rules for the transition of letters from one to the other." Unfortunately, he wrote in Danish, a language little known outside Denmark; hence his essay got little publicity until it was printed in German in 1818. Another contribution he made to linguistics by example: he was a pioneer field linguist, traveling from Denmark through Sweden, Finland, Russia, Persia, and India, gathering his own field notes from native speakers instead of relying upon written texts, as did many of his contemporaries.

The Germans patriotically date the birth of comparative philology from 1816, with the publication of Franz Bopp's work with the formidable title of *On the Conjugational System of the Sanskrit Language in Comparison with that of Greek, Latin, Persian and the Germanic Languages*. Small wonder that many consider

[1] The Indo-European language group is the largest language family in the world, comprising most of the languages of Europe, plus many of India and other countries. English belongs to the Indo-European family.

Bopp the greatest of the founders of modern linguistics. Probably Bopp's most important contribution was a reinforcement of Jones' brief statement to the effect that Sanskrit, as well as Greek and Latin, "have sprung from some common source, which, perhaps, no longer exists." Many philologists of the time, such as Schlegel, believed that Sanskrit itself was the parent language. Said Bopp, "I do not believe that the Greek, Latin, and other European languages are to be considered as derived from the Sanskrit. . . . I feel rather inclined to consider them altogether as subsequent variations of one original tongue, which, however, the Sanskrit has preserved more perfect than its kindred dialects."

The third of the "Big Three" was Jakob Grimm. This German professor, bachelor, and romantic was also one of the compilers of *Grimms' Fairy Tales*. In *Germanic Grammar* (1822), he enlarged upon Rask's statement regarding "the transition of letters from one [language] to the other" by providing more data and systematizing it, thus demonstrating the complex of phonetic, or sound, changes by which practically all the Germanic consonants developed from corresponding Indo-European consonants. So regular are the phonetic shifts in his lists that he evolved a theory to account for the phenomenon, a statement that later, thanks to Max Müller, was labeled GRIMM'S LAW, although sweating students in language classes often refer to it as the "grim law." A few exceptions to his "law" bedeviled scholars for half a century, until Karl Verner carefully traced out the cause for these apparent discrepancies and accounted for them, still under the general thesis of Grimm's law. (This sound-shift will be dealt with in Chapter 4.)

A final note on Grimm: his work as a compiler of fairy tales was more extensive and influential than the collection of tales would suggest. As a folklorist, he broke from the classical philologists—who concerned themselves primarily with Greek, Latin, and the Bible—and collected and studied ballads, legends, superstitions, and other orally transmitted literature which are so valuable to linguists. (For example, earlier forms of English are reflected in old ballads which contain words such as "deef" for "deaf," "clumb" for "climbed," "eaten and drunken" for "eaten and drunk." And how long would "posies" last were it not for "Ring Around the Rosies"?) Grimm recognized that written literature is but a small and incomplete sampling of the mentality of a people.

So far we can see the contributions of these earlier investigators toward our modern concepts in linguistics: language as a system, the changing nature of language, the relationship among languages, languages as "dialects" of a family, and many others.

The work of the first half of the nineteenth century was summed up by Friedrich Maximilian (Max) Müller, whom we met in Chapter 1. Müller was a pupil of Bopp and an excellent student of Sanskrit. In 1861 he began a series of lectures at Oxford entitled *Lessons in the Science of Language*, in which he reviewed the comparative studies of the preceding years. Not generally regarded as profound or original, Müller did succeed in popularizing the science of linguistics. While Verner's work in straightening out apparent discrepancies in Grimm's law of phonetic shift is regarded as a beginning point for a new school of linguists known as the *Junggrammatiker* ("young grammarians"), Müller anticipated them by nearly a score of years in voicing what became, in effect, one of their rallying cries: "All becomes clear and intelligible in the light of comparative grammar; anomalies vanish, exceptions prove the rule!"

While other names appear in more comprehensive studies of nineteenth-century linguistics, we will limit ourselves to just one more name before meeting the *Junggrammatiker*.

August Schleicher was a linguist who was strongly influenced by Charles Darwin's theory of natural selection. Applying organic development to languages, he introduced the family tree to illustrate how a number of languages are the result of dividing and subdividing from an original language. (The family tree is discussed in Chapter 4.) And certainly Schleicher's own statement describes quite well the purpose of historical linguistics:

> Grammar forms one part of the science of language: this science is itself a part of the natural history of Man. Its method

is in substance that of natural science generally; it consists in accurate investigation of our object and in conclusions founded upon that investigation. One of the chief problems of the science of language is the inquiry into, and description of, the classes of language or speech-stems, that is, of the languages which are derived from one and the same original tongue, and the arrangement of these classes according to a natural system. (From the *Introduction* to the *Compendium of the Comparative Grammar of the Indo-European, Sanskrit, Greek and Latin Languages*, 1871.)

Now, who were the *Junggrammatiker?* They were a group of German scholars, mainly younger men, who, in the time-honored tradition of Young Turks, noisily proclaimed that their linguistic elders were reactionary while they themselves were progressive. More specifically, Karl Brugmann was inspired to take violent issue with his previous masters and their linguistic concepts. So he moved to Leipzig, where he became a professor and founded a new school of linguistics. His group was labeled DIE JUNGGRAMMATIKER, also known as the NEOGRAMMARIANS, and included such scholars as August Leskien, who was responsible for their battle cry: "Sound-laws have no exception." The American Leonard Bloomfield later joined the group as a young student.

Their purpose was to have linguistics accepted as a natural science. Their method was to borrow Isaac Newton's model of a closed system in physics: that is, a solid linguistic theory could admit no exceptions. And from Darwin's theory of evolution they picked up the organic analogy of developing forms following absolute laws. Verner had recently brought out his clarification of the "exceptions" in Grimm's law, thus giving a basis for the new thesis that sound-laws have no exception. There was strong objection from the opposite camp, mainly to the effect that it is invalid to establish a new science strictly by analogy, particularly by comparing it with the theory of the evolution of man. Also, one of the characteristics of the scientific method is predictability. How could anyone predict the future of language?

As we have seen so far, practically all ideas are based in one way or another on earlier ideas, and those of the *Jung-*

grammatiker were no exception. A glance back at our note on Müller shows that he had already anticipated the basic premise of the "new" credo. For that matter, Schleicher and Grimm and others had furnished much of the data and suggestions the *Junggrammatiker* adopted. In fact, Ferdinand de Saussure, who seems to have involuntarily exploded the whole new movement into being, was quite generous in acknowledging the contributions of other nineteenth-century linguists. He gave credit to an American linguist, William Dwight Whitney, for giving the first impetus to the new approach to language study, that of searching out the principles that control the life of languages.

To sum up: the *Junggrammatiker*, as comparative linguists, were mainly concerned with comparing Indo-European languages historically, and reconstructing Sanskrit—but, it should be noted, still using the classical Latin grammar for description. Consequently, they were heavy on rules. And their concern was strictly with linguistic artifacts, and not at all with people, those producers of language. To paraphrase Jespersen, they lost sight of the forest in their preoccupation with "dead leaves."

Lest it be supposed that the comparative movement was strictly German, we must point out that other Europeans (and Americans) were involved. Graziadio Ascoli, an Italian scholar, published in 1870 a paper on the phonetic changes in Sanskrit, ending forever the long-held notion that Sanskrit was identical with the PROTO-INDO-EUROPEAN language (the ancestor of all Indo-European languages), or even the language closest to it. Working in the same area were the Dane Vilhelm Thomsen and the Swiss Saussure.

Saussure is generally considered to be the founder of modern linguistics. A classmate of Brugmann and Leskien, he was only twenty-two when he published his stimulating, highly original paper on Indo-European phonetics, one of the studies which caused Brugmann to break from the conservative group and start his own school of linguistic research. Saussure's influence was most strongly felt through his lectures at the University of Geneva. After he died in 1913, his devoted students collated and edited all their notes from his lectures, and published them as the *Cours de Linguistique Générale.* The work was translated into German, Japanese, Spanish, and Russian, and in 1959 into English. In the *Cours* Saussure states, politely as always, that the *Junggrammatiker* did not solve all language problems, that the fundamental problems of general linguistics were still to be solved. According to Saussure, the scope of linguistics should be

> a) to describe and trace the history of all observable languages, which amounts to tracing the history of families of languages and reconstructing as far as possible the mother language of each family;
>
> b) to determine the forces that are permanently and universally at work in all languages, and to deduce the general laws to which all specific historical phenomena can be reduced; and
>
> c) to delimit and define itself. (From *Course in General Linguistics.* New York: McGraw-Hill, 1966. P. 6.)

Among Saussure's contributions is a distinction between DIACHRONIC (historical) and SYNCHRONIC linguistics, the second being the intensive study of a language at a given moment in history. (The *Junggrammatiker* had insisted entirely on diachronic analyses of languages.) His exposition of synchronic analysis led to the school of descriptive linguistics which developed around the work of Leonard Bloomfield in America.

Since Saussure there has developed the "Copenhagen School," under the guidance of Louis Hjelmslev; the "Prague School," under Prince Nikolai Trubetzkoy and Roman Jakobson; and the "London School," under J. R. Firth. However, we will restrict ourselves to a discussion of the "American School" and some contributions of a few of its noted linguists.

Linguistics in America

Another German, an immigrant scholar named Franz Boas, might be said to have started the scientific study of descriptive linguistics in the United States. He came primarily as an anthropologist, first to the Pacific Northwest, where he studied the Indians of that region. Convinced that to understand the culture of another people one must understand the language, he became a linguist. Boas brought a new approach to language analysis. Instead of imposing grammatical categories of European-based languages upon the various Indian languages, Boas realized that each language has its own peculiar and distinctive phonetic and grammatical system. Thus was Saussure's synchronic analysis applied in America. Boas' major publication is the *Handbook of American Indian Languages* (1911). However, his greatest contribution to American linguistics was his teaching. He emphasized the collecting of data in the field, then generalizing from that data rather than from preconceived notions of cultural philosophy and structures of other languages. Boas became the first professor of anthropology at Columbia University.

Next in line is Edward Sapir, who became associated with Boas at Columbia in 1904. Like Boas, Sapir was also an immigrant from Germany, but he had come to the United States at the age of five. He was majoring in Germanic studies when he came under the influence of the older man. Excited by Boas' approach to field linguistics, Sapir became an enthusiastic student of American Indian languages and an expert in many of them. Not only did he publish articles on Indian languages ranging from the Kwakiutl of the North to the Nahuatl of the South, but he also dealt with Chinese and some African languages. Like Boas, Sapir's greatest influence was in his teaching (first at the University of Chicago, then at Yale) and in the publication of his book, *Language* (1921). It would be impossible to list here all the insights presented or hinted at in Sapir's little book. As well as considering basic linguistic principles in analyzing language, he also discusses the possibility of thought without language, still a knotty problem, and the natural drift of language. Language has a drift; if there were no breaking up into dialects, a language would still move away from its original form so drastically as to form a new language. His book also contains the hint from which developed the Sapir-Whorf hypothesis, which will be discussed later.

Probably better known than Boas and Sapir is Leonard Bloomfield. A contemporary of Sapir, Bloomfield also made a thorough study of Germanic languages before becoming interested in American Indian languages, a turn which resulted in his study of general principles underlying all languages. All of his findings and conclusions are concentrated in his book *Language* (1933), a work which is regarded by many as "the Bible" in establishing the American School of linguistics. The book is undeniably a masterpiece. Written with beautiful clarity, it includes a critical synthesis of earlier linguists and their work, but mainly it contains Bloomfield's own original contributions, based on extensive and intensive field work, in the tradition of Boas and Sapir. Neogrammarian in many ways, he followed a line of study set up by Grimm and developed by Saussure, beginning with sound-change. More than any of his predecessors, Bloomfield made a science of linguistics.

Bloomfield died in 1949. But long before his death the structuralist school, which he inspired, had proliferated, producing scores of intelligent—some brilliant—scholars and researchers. World War II added impetus to linguistic research by the demand for thousands of nonnative speakers of what had formerly been considered exotic languages. Even the familiar languages such as French, Spanish, and German were examined from a new angle: What was the quickest way of getting basic structure across to the learner? Vocabulary could come in more gradually. Consequently, all this concentration on structure resulted in a mistaken notion that meaning was being completely disregarded by modern linguists.

Nothing could be further from the truth, protested Charles C. Fries, himself one of the great teachers of the twentieth century. And shortly before he died, Bloomfield, too, insisted that such a school—linguists who study language structure with no regard for meaning—did not exist. Even phonology (the study of speech production), he said, involves the consideration of meaning.

The most recent event of major importance in the history of linguistics is the advancement of Noam Chomsky's ideas and theories in *generative grammar*. The movement, for such it has become, began in 1957 with the publication of Chomsky's *Syntactic Structures*. Most laymen found the book all but impossible to read, and many linguists had to read it and re-read it to understand what Chomsky was getting at. Since that time a spate of books has been printed, explaining and simplifying the principles of the new grammar, called by some *transformational*, by others *generative-transformational*, and by still others something else. Either term, transformational or generative, is appropriate. The potential of this approach to language study is tremendous, and in one form or another it is being used more every day. There are still some linguists who are reluctant to grant it such force, while on the other side are those enthusiasts who feel it can eventually answer all the problems of language.

Much of what Chomsky has advanced is, ironically, quite old, as he himself says. However, his own genius and synthesizing powers have created from a vast amount of knowledge a new tool for linguistic work. One goal of the traditional, or classical, grammarian was to account for what kind of knowledge the mature user of a language must have in order to construct correctly formed sentences and to interpret new sentences which he hears. This has been the purpose of Chomsky, to construct a grammar which accounts for the ability of a native speaker to form grammatical sentences he has never spoken before, and to interpret (as grammatical or ungrammatical) sentences he has never heard before.

To briefly illustrate a basic difference in philosophy between Boas and Chomsky: Boas was extremely cautious about imposing ready-made, European-language structures on a body of Indian-language data. He insisted that *only* the collected material itself be used for analysis and description. The high point of this procedure was reached by Fries near the midpoint of this century. Instead of collecting written data from largely literary sources, Fries tapped telephone lines—shades of the FBI!—and collected a tremendous body of utterances in spoken English. From this material he derived basic sentence structures. But as Chomsky points out, such a procedure limits the investigator. Instead of deriving rules just for this limited collection of utterances, the investigator should try to discover underlying rules which would generate an infinite number of grammatically acceptable utterances in the target language, above and beyond those collected by the investigator.

The field linguist today follows just such a procedure. As he collects and arranges his notes in the target language, he works up tentative rules, then tests them by trying out utterances on his native informants, utterances that he has not heard before, but which he has himself generated from his tentative rules. He gets laughed at often enough by native speakers when he makes mistakes, but he keeps on testing.

The generative linguist is intrigued by the enormous amount of data available to any native speaker, by the specific skills that a child brings unconsciously to language learning, by the *competence*, or latent capability, of the speaker as compared to his *performance* when he talks. So we find that modern linguists are returning to certain of the philosophical questions pondered by the thinkers of ancient times. But instead of saying that the study of language has come full circle, back to its starting point, a statement which would imply little or no progress, we may more aptly describe the history of linguistics as a widening spiral ever coming back on itself, but ever increasing its diameter.

The fact is, with such a vastly expanded interest in linguistics today, it is virtually impossible for one scholar to master all aspects of the discipline. For example, a teacher working in *applied linguistics*, say the teaching of English as a second language, is not necessarily versed in *historical linguistics*, the study of the developments in languages across time. Nor does the teacher necessarily know all about *psycholinguistics*, the psychological aspects of language, nor *semantics*, the science of meaning. Obviously, though, the more he knows of these related areas the better off he is. We still have those students and scholars who give most of their attention to descriptive linguistics. We also still have philologists, who are primarily concerned with examining and dating old texts. All these areas of language study contribute to a general theory of language.

FOR FURTHER READING

Bloomfield, Leonard, *Language*. New York: Holt, Rinehart and Winston, 1965.

Dinneen, Francis P., *An Introduction to General Linguistics*. New York: Holt, Rinehart and Winston, 1967.

Hughes, John P., *The Science of Language*, 2nd ed. New York: Random House, 1964.

Lehmann, Winfred P., ed., *A Reader in Nineteenth-Century Historical Indo-European Linguistics*. Bloomington: Indiana University Press, 1967.

Pedersen, Holger, *The Discovery of Language: Linguistic Science in the Nineteenth Century*. Bloomington: Indiana University Press, 1967.

Waterman, John T., *Perspectives in Linguistics*. Chicago: University of Chicago Press, 1963.

Sitch-tche-na-ko, the goddess Thinking Woman, created a man and a woman from clay, and taught them language. The next formed couple she taught a different language, and the next couple she taught still another language. So we have different languages on earth.

Pueblo Indian myth

And the whole earth was of one language, and of one speech. . . . And the Lord said, Behold the people is one, and they have all one language. . . . Let us go down and there confound their language, that they may not understand one another's speech. So the Lord scattered them abroad from thence upon the face of the earth.

Genesis 11:1, 6–8

3

LANGUAGES AND DIALECTS

Some fundamentalists believe that the story from Genesis is literal, and that the original language was Hebrew. Some linguists also have held the belief in the *monogenesis* of language, that in the beginning there was only one language—but it wasn't Hebrew. In the early eighteenth century Leibniz theorized that all languages came from a single proto-language. In the following century Max Müller argued for *polygenesis*, or several original languages. His belief was that proto-man split up geographically before animal sounds had evolutionized into human speech; hence human languages were different from one another from the very beginning of man. More recently Morris Swadesh has postulated twelve basic groups of world languages and has suggested that quite likely all these languages ultimately derived from a single ancestor.

The Languages of the World

Apart from theorizing, what do we actually know about the languages of the world and their family relationships? In 1970, an international symposium was held to organize a survey to classify and describe all the languages of the world. It would be guessing to say when the survey will be completed. For now, it is generally accepted that the world's languages number something like three thousand, though opinions vary considerably on either side of this number. Yet only a tiny fraction of these languages is spoken natively by the great majority of the world's population. In fact, only six—Chinese, English, Hindi-Urdu, Spanish, Russian, and German—are spoken by well over a hundred million native speakers apiece, totaling more than a billion people. A vastly greater number of languages are spoken by less than a thousand speakers each.

To further complicate communication among peoples, these three thousand languages are modified into an awesome number of dialects, or variants of the languages. For example, India has fourteen recognized languages, plus scores of dialects. Hindi is officially the state language of India, but since less than half the population speaks this language, government and business must be conducted in English as a LINGUA FRANCA, or working language for people of different linguistic backgrounds. The Soviet Union has sixteen official languages, and numerous dialects. A similar diversity of languages exists among the American Indians. When the eighteen tribes of Pueblo Indians of the Southwest come together in their All-Pueblo Councils, business is conducted in English because most of the members do not understand each other's languages.

In attempting to present even a sketchy outline of the world's languages, a researcher must admit to the obsolescence of his effort at the outset. About the best that a survey of the languages of the world can do at the present moment is to report the data available.

As of 1971, the world's population was over 3.5 billion, and growing. The language spoken by the most people, Mandarin Chinese, was gaining approximately 14 million speakers a year. Table 3-1 gives the fifteen leading languages and the chief countries in which they are spoken.

TABLE 3-1

The Leading Languages

Language	Number of speakers (in millions)	Chief countries
Mandarin	515	China
English	265	USA, United Kingdom
Hindi-Urdu	185	India, Pakistan
Spanish	145	Spain, Latin America
Russian	135	USSR
German	100	Germany, Austria
Japanese	95	Japan
Arabic	90	Middle East, North Africa
Bengali	85	Pakistan, India
Portuguese	85	Portugal, Brazil
French	65	France, Canada
Cantonese	55	China
Italian	55	Italy
Wu	55	China
Fukienese	50	China, Taiwan

The language recorded as having the least number of speakers is Andamanese, which is spoken in the Andaman Islands of India. It has approximately four hundred speakers.

The known languages of the world may be broadly classified

under the family groups shown in Table 3-2—with the clear understanding that such classification is susceptible to constant revision as more and more data is collected.

TABLE 3-2

Language Families of the World

1. *Indo-European.* Includes English, Spanish, Portuguese, French, Hindi, Urdu, Russian, Italian, German, and others.
2. *Sino-Tibetan.* Includes the several Chinese languages, Thai, Burmese, Tibetan, and others. Probably does not include Mon-Khmer, to which Vietnamese is related.
3. *Semito-Hamitic.* Includes Arabic, Hebrew, Ethiopic, Hausa, Berber, Somali, and others.
4. *African.* May be divided into two broad classes: Northern, or Sudanic, with approximately 450 languages, including Fala, Mandingo, Twi-Fante, Fon, Yoruba, Ibo, and others; Southern, or Bantu, with approximately 250 languages, including Kongo, Swahili, Kikuyu, Ruanda, Zulu, Xhosa, and others.
5. *Japanese.* Some linguists connect Korean with Japanese.
6. *Other Asian languages.* Includes Korean, Ainu, and others.
7. *Ural-Altaic.* Includes Finnish, Estonian, Hungarian, Turkish, Mongolian, Manchurian, and others.
8. *Malayo-Polynesian.* Includes Malay, Javanese, Balinese, Visayan, Tagalog, Ilocano, Fiji, Samoan, Maori, Tongan, Chamorro, Tahitian, Hawaiian, and others.
9. *Papuan.* Includes the languages of New Guinea and other South Pacific islands.
10. *Australian.* Includes Bushman and others.
11. *Khoisan.* Includes Hottenot, Bushman (African), Hatsa, and Sandawe.
12. *Caucasian.* Includes Abkhaz, Circassian, Georgian, and others.

13. *Dravidian*. Includes Telugu, Tamil, Kanarese, and Malayalam.
14. *Basque*. A separate language, unrelated (so far) to any other known language. Considered by some to be directly descended from a cave-age language.
15. *Amerindian*. North American languages are generally classified under six or eight families, which include Algonquian, Athapaskan, Uto-Aztecan, Penutian, Hokan, Muskhogean, Siouan, and perhaps others. The Central and South American languages are presently being worked on intensively. Possibly, as some linguists conjecture, they truly belong to the same families as those of North America. They are generally grouped under Quechua, Aymara, Guarani, Arawak, Carib, Maya, and others.

Language, Dialect, and Communication

Before going any further in the discussion of language families and language change, it is necessary to have an understanding of the difference between LANGUAGE and DIALECT. First, let it be said that there is not always a clear-cut distinction between the two. One of the most common—and valid—characteristics of a language is mutual intelligibility. That is, in a particular linguistic community, or language group, everyone understands everyone else. They speak the same language. In the adjacent community the speech is so different that it is not understood by the first community. The two communities speak two different languages. An example would be France and Germany, or the United States and Mexico, or Greece and Italy, or Korea and China. Within a single language community, particularly if it is large, there will probably be subgroups who speak the common language, but with differences in pronunciation, vocabulary, or other linguistic components. But as long as the different subgroups still understand each other, their language variations are called dialects.

The distinction between language and dialect is not always such a simple matter. Mutual understanding may depend upon such factors as intelligence and education. Lack of understanding may be due to culturally and emotionally conditioned attitudes toward "outsiders," as, for instance, a feeling of superiority. The ancient Greeks' term for non-Greeks—"barbarians," or "babblers"—displayed such linguistic chauvinism. A minimum estimate of the number of languages in New Guinea, an island of impenetrable jungle, mountains, and valleys, is over a hundred. Not only the rugged terrain contributes to this communication barrier; an intense intertribal hostility has rendered what undoubtedly were formerly dialects into mutually unintelligible languages.

At this point a definition should be made clear. All too often the linguistic term "dialect" carries a sense of belittling. Many people react to the term emotionally, feeling that a dialect is an inferior brand of speech. Any dialect, as long as it serves its purpose of communication, is perfectly honorable and "correct." Generally, however, one dialect in a speech community of two or more dialects becomes the dominant dialect, or the official speech for that language community. In fourteenth- and fifteenth-century England, several dialects of English were spoken, but because of such dynamics as trade, government, and educational institutions, London became the center of power and influence, and consequently the London dialect gradually became the standard speech of England. Similarly, the dialect of Île-de-France gained ascendancy over Norman, Picard, and Champenois French. In Italy, the Tuscan dialect became standard Italian over the dialects of Sicily, Lombardy, and Bologna. In China, the official language is Mandarin, since that is the dialect spoken in Peking, the capital city.

The northern province of Eritrea was the ancient seat of government and culture in Ethiopia. The natives of this province are Tigre, speakers of Tigrinya. Addis Abbaba, the modern capital of Ethiopia, is in the south-central part, and the lineage of the king is Amharic; therefore, the official language of the country is Amharic. Under the current bilingual-education program in the north, beginning schoolchildren are taught in both dialects. Basically, the two systems of speech are dialects; that is, while they have certain vocabulary differences, certain pronunciation differences, and considerable rhetorical differences, the speakers are able to understand each other. Yet among some of the older people, certain feelings of pride, or class distinction, or other social attitudes establish a communication barrier so impenetrable that the two dialects become in effect two languages. Amharic speech is often very flowery, full of subtle suggestions and double meanings. Many Tigre complain that they cannot understand such rhetorical embroidery. But the Amhara do not see such usage as being too flowery and subtle. They maintain that one does not speak the language properly unless one uses it in every way conceivable.

Among the Spanish-Americans of New Mexico, Arizona, Texas, and California are at least four varieties of Spanish, but the speakers generally understand each other in spite of vocabulary and pronunciation differences. However, in small communities in northern New Mexico are some inhabitants who speak only their own particular dialect of Spanish. They have rarely if ever traveled far from their birthplaces; they have not been educated in standard Spanish; and often they have received very little formal education at all. With such a restriction of intercultural relations or development, they sometimes find it quite difficult to communicate with speakers of other Spanish dialects, such as visitors from Mexico. On the other hand, a well-educated and culturally sophisticated citizen of any Central or South American country would be able to talk with an educated and sophisticated citizen of any other Latin country of the Southern Hemisphere, even with a Brazilian, a speaker of Portuguese.

A rather extreme case of culture shock plus communication breakdown involved a friend of mine, a linguist who learned Japanese during World War II and was sent to Japan with the occupation forces. His Japanese was quite fluent, and he was easily understood by the urban Japanese around Tokyo. But on one occasion he was sent to a northern province to carry out some sort of mission among a rural and unsophisticated community, none of whose citizens had yet seen any Americans. My friend addressed them in Japanese, but to his dismay they seemed not to understand him at all. They only stared at him. Then it occurred to him what the problem was: he was blond and blue-eyed, and the shock of hearing their own language from one so completely non-Japanese in appearance had simply blocked their understanding.

In one sense we can say that there is no English language as such, but only dialects of English forming a speech community subsumed under the heading of "native speakers of English." To say that British English is more "correct" than American English simply because England is the homeland is completely erroneous. The historical homeland of the English language was not England but rather northern Germany. The English spoken in Canada, the United States, England, Australia, New Zealand, India, and South Africa has distinct differences in vocabulary and pronunciation and, to a far lesser degree, in grammar. A "garbage can" in one country is a "dustbin" in another; "aluminum" in one country is "aluminium" in another; speakers in one country say, "The Assembly are ready," while speakers in another country say, "The Assembly is ready." There are no valid grounds for calling one form more correct than the other.

Even within a dialect we may have regional accents and grammatical and vocabulary differences which constitute subdialects. In the United States as well as in other countries throughout the world, LINGUISTIC ATLASES have been made to classify and localize these subdialects. The linguistic geographer records the speech items which characterize a particular region, then draws lines on a map to indicate where one set of speech items ends and another begins. Such lines are called ISOGLOSSES, and they resemble the lines drawn on weather maps. For example, to demarcate the Southern Dialect Area, a line would be drawn on a map of the United States from a point along the Maryland shore, southward across the Virginia Piedmont, the eastern parts of North Carolina, South Carolina, Georgia, and Florida, then westward along the Gulf Coast. Within this area you would hear such grammatical items as "It wan't (*or* weren't) me"; vocabulary items such as "harp" for "harmonica"; pronunciation characteristics such as "Miz" for "Mrs.," and frequent loss of "r" except before vowels: "foah" for "four," "heah" for "here," and "sulfuh" for "sulfur."

As well as the Southern Dialect Area, the United States is further subdivided into the Northern, the Northern Midland, and the Southern Midland dialect areas (see Figure 3-1). In the Northern area, most speakers would say, "He isn't to home," for "He isn't at home"; and "dove" for "dived." A "bucket" is a "pail" in the Northern area, and "weatherboards" are "clapboards." The word "because" is pronounced like "becuz." Throughout the Midland areas you would hear, "I'll wait on you," for "I'll wait for you"; and "I want off," for "I want to get off." A "pail" is a "bucket" in the Midland areas, as well as in the Southern, and a "frying pan" is generally

FIGURE 3-1

Isogloss Map

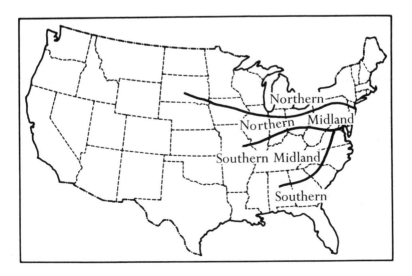

a "skillet." Also in the Midlands, "Mary" and "dairy" are pronounced "Merry" and "derry."

Cultural and Social Dialects

For a large nation, the United States is moving faster than most smaller countries toward a blending and fusing of regional dialects and subdialects. Several forces contribute to this leveling, the first being the extreme mobility of American families. Parents move their families back and forth across the country as they transfer from one job location to another. According to Alvin Toffler, author of *Future Shock*, between March 1967 and March 1968, 36.6 million Americans changed their places of residence; and this is an annual happening. Children, being particularly adaptable linguistically, adjust to—and adopt—the speech characteristics of the area in which they find themselves. Even the mobility of schoolteachers is a force in speech molding. Another force is the prevalence of television and movies. Certain programs sometimes emphasize regional subdialects, especially the accents; but usually the programs project a more generalized speech pattern than some viewer-listeners are accustomed to, thus subtly influencing the speech characteristics of these particular listeners.

While regional dialects and subdialects are being leveled, other forces continue to maintain communication barriers. Social dialects may reflect different levels of education, wealth, social position, job or profession, or even the speaker's home location (city, suburbs, rural, and so on). Cultural background or national origin also makes an impression on speech patterns.

One cultural dialect which is gaining increasing attention is Black English. Originally this dialect was held to be a "broken" English developed by illiterate slaves, but dialectologists now are finding many patterns of the original African languages in it. Many early pronouncements regarding Black English are being invalidated. For example, H. L. Mencken, in his well-known

The American Language, claims that the Negro dialect "was a vague and artificial lingo which had little relation to the actual speech of Southern blacks." As a matter of fact, closer studies of Black English are revealing a very formalized grammar, the rules of which are followed intuitively by its native speakers.

Modern researchers generally agree that the greatest differences between Black English and Standard American English lie in pronunciation. A few early writers of American dialects were able to represent accurately the spoken Black English of their day. One of these was Joel Chandler Harris, author of the *Uncle Remus* stories, from which the following excerpt is taken:

> Well, atter Brer Fox done git rested fum keepin' out er de way er Mr. Dog, en sorter ketch up wid his rations, he say ter hisse'f dat he be dog his cats ef he don't slorate ole Brer Rabbit ef it take 'im a mont.

With the black literary movement known as the Harlem Renaissance in the early part of this century, black writers began to go more and more into their own culture for material. This included the use of dialect. Arna Bontemps, a twentieth-century black writer, transcribed the spoken language of a black couple in this passage from one of his stories, "A Summer Tragedy":

> "I reckon you'll have to he'p me wid this heah bow tie, baby," he said meekly. "Dog if I can hitch it up."
>
> "You oughta could do a heap mo' wid a thing like that'n me—beingst as you got yo' good sight."
>
> "Looks like I oughta could," he admitted. "But ma fingers is gone democrat on me. I get all mixed up in the looking glass an' can't tell wicha way to twist the devilish thing." (From Abraham Chapman, ed., *Black Voices*. New York: New American Library, 1968.)

That the same pronunciation characteristics still continue in Black English is demonstrated in these few lines from a taped narration of the "Three Little Pigs" by an eleven-year-old black student. His improvisation was taped in 1969.

> He huff an' 'e puff an' 'e tuff an' 'e ruff an' 'e cou'n' knock de house down. An' he say, "Li'l pig, I know somewhey some appuz [apples] at."
> He say, "Whey um?"
> "Down to duh Millah Hi' Li' [Miller High Life]."
> An' 'e say, 'e say, "Whut time you goin'?"
> He say, "'Bout one uhclock."
> An' 'e wen' uh picked uz appuz, an' uh ol' wolf came. (From Susan H. Houston, *Child Black English in North Florida: A Sociolinguistic Examination.* Atlanta, Ga.: Southeastern Education Laboratory [September 1969]. Pp. 50–52.)

Among the grammatical characteristics of Black English, one of the most prominent is the "invariant *be.*" In the *Uncle Remus* passage on p. 51, the narrator says, ". . . he *be* dog his cats ef. . . ." Today, Black English speakers say: "It be raining today." "He be's late every day." "Where Floyd? He be on the playground." In the question "Where Floyd?" you will notice the omission of the verb "is." This omission occurs regularly in Black English where Standard English would use a contraction: "Where's Floyd?"

To go into more detailed analysis of the characteristics of Black English would exceed the scope of this book. However, a number of enlightening studies, such as that of J. L. Dillard (listed at the end of the chapter), present excellent details on the subject.

Until recently—and even now, among some individuals— the use of dialect, particularly the Black English dialect, was regarded with disfavor and embarrassment. Today, however, students are being taught that their particular dialect is as good as any other, but that a mastery of Standard English provides them with a wider range of communication outside their own speech community. Thus, an increasing number of American blacks are quite proud of their BIDIALECTALISM—that is, their ability to converse in both Standard English and Black English.

The same unfavorable cultural-linguistic situation prevailed in Hawaii until recently. The children of the islands, coming from mixed backgrounds, spoke Hawaiian Pidgin (see Chapter 9), a nonstandard dialect of English. They were often scolded and sometimes punished in school for speaking pidgin instead of Standard English. After World War II, however, a wider understanding and appreciation of linguistics resulted in different approaches to language training. The local dialect was no longer looked upon with disfavor. In fact, today a control of Hawaiian Pidgin is a mark of status, and like the educated black of the Mainland, the Hawaiian who speaks both Hawaiian Pidgin and Standard English sees himself as bidialectal. One of my students at the University of Hawaii took great delight in writing *Little Red Riding Hood* in pidgin for me. The following excerpt is from her paper:

> Once upon a time there was one kid name Little Red Riding Hood. Man, she was some porky-looking kid. One day her old lady went go tell her, "Sister, you need some exercise, so go take this basket of poi and lomi salmon to your Tutu." So Red Riding Hood went take the basket to Tutu's. She walk so much that her big luau feet got real sore. She then went rest underneath one lauhala tree. While she was resting, one wolf came along. He was some ugly, skinny bugga, one sight for the sore eyes. His opu was empty, and the smell from the wahine's basket was making him mo' hungry. . . .

The generation gap contributes its own impediment to communication. The youth protest of the late 1960s and early '70s impelled sociologist George Steiner to comment:

> Changes of idiom between generations are a normal part of social history. . . . [But] what is occurring now is new: it is an attempt at a total break. The mumble of the dropout, the silence of the teen-ager in the enemy house of his parents, are meant to destroy. Deliberate violence is being done to those primary ties of identity and social cohesion produced by a common language. (From "A Future Literacy," *The Atlantic Monthly* [August 1971]. Pp. 41–44.)

The drug cult, too, has produced its own speech patterns which comprise a dialect that is sometimes incomprehensible to the nonmember. And the underworld has its own dialect, consisting both of strange words and of familiar words used in a totally different context or with different meanings from standard usage.

Nor is this a recent phenomenon. In Renaissance England there were writers who examined with great interest the different dialects they heard spoken around them, particularly in London. In *Lantern and Candlelight* (1608), Thomas Dekker gives the following example of "canting," the substandard dialect of the London underworld:

> Stow you, bene cofe, and cut benar whids, and bing we to Romeville to nip a bung. So shall we have lower for the boozing ken, and when we bing back to the Deuce-a-ville we will filch some duds off the ruffmans or mill the ken for a lag of duds.

Dekker translates this as:

> Hold your peace, good fellow, and speak better words, and go we to London to cut a purse. So shall we have money for the alehouse, and when we come back into the country we will filch some clothes from the hedges or rob the house for a buck of clothes.

We have already pointed out that the deciding factor between what constitutes a language and what a dialect is often not an objective one. That is, no clear-cut line can be drawn to indicate at what point different but understandable dialects become incomprehensible languages. The ability to comprehend is heavily dependent upon individual intelligence, emotional attitudes, and sophistication—generally acquired through travel. Of these three factors, probably the first is of least importance, given at least reasonably normal intelligence. That is, a person who has earned a Ph.D. (in a nonlinguistic field) is not necessarily more qualified to understand other dialects and languages than a high school graduate. In fact, a highly educated person might find his analytical approach to understanding a strange speech a handicap; he might be so intent upon analyzing the structure of the utterance that he misses entirely the substance of the message. A classic, if possibly exaggerated, example is "Buck Fanshaw's Funeral" in *Roughing It*, by Mark Twain. Scotty Briggs, a roughneck Western miner, approaches a newly arrived Eastern minister:

> "Are you the duck that runs the gospel-mill next door?"
>
> "Am I the—pardon me, I believe I do not understand."
>
> "The boys thought maybe you would give us a lift, if we'd tackle you—that is, if I've got the rights of it and you are the head clerk of the doxology-works next door."
>
> "I am the shepherd in charge of the flock whose fold is next door."
>
> "The which?"
>
> "The spiritual adviser of the little company of believers whose sanctuary adjoins these premises."
>
> Scotty scratched his head, reflected a moment, and then said: "You ruther hold over me, pard. I reckon I can't call that hand. Ante and pass the buck."
>
> "How? I beg pardon. What did I understand you to say?"
>
> "You see, one of the boys has passed in his checks, and we want to give him a good send-off."

On the other hand, the educated person may have certain advantages. If he has a wide vocabulary, he might make out fairly well in other languages akin to his own through a COGNATE familiarity—recognition, that is, of relationship between words in two languages. An American who knows that "pediatrician" means a doctor who treats children might recognize the word *paidi* in Greece as meaning "child." And a Spaniard or Mexican in France would have no difficulty with *blanc*; it is almost the same as his own word for "white": *blanco*.

The emotional attitude is probably the most important factor in comprehending alien speech patterns. A sympathetic person would strain for the sense of the message more than for the grammatical structure. Motivation in the form of desire, which is a part of the emotional attitude, is the key to under-standing and learning any language. On the other hand, a strong dislike toward a language—or toward the speakers of that language—will establish a block to understanding the language. This emotional rejection has a spectrum of its own, ranging from a mild feeling of superiority to insanity. The latter extreme is represented by the autistic-schizophrenic patient who creates his own private language, a code used for protection and secrecy rather than for communication. In the same way, it is entirely possible for a particular culture to use its own language or dialect as a security device, a form of ego protection.

The third factor, lack of sophistication, is more innocent than the others in its ignorance (not stupidity). For people who have had little or no contact with other cultures and their speech systems, to encounter an alien communication system would be just about as great a culture shock as to encounter a saucerful of little green men from Mars. Most likely, it would be even more of a shock, because the unsophisticated would rather expect a different language system from the little green men, while a strange set of sounds from a people who are clearly also human beings just wouldn't register fully. "Why don't they speak English like us?" (Or French? Or Chinese? Or Urdu? Or Swahili?)

Given reasonable intelligence, the most important aid to learning another language is motivation. Motivation may spring from a person falling in love with someone of another language and culture. (Thousands of war brides learned English with varying degrees of fluency rather quickly.) It may spring from a simple desire to improve one's economic position by learning another language. Or, as in World War II, learning another language becomes a necessary tactic in warfare.

In addition to languages and dialects, we have IDIOLECTS. An idiolect is the set of individual speech characteristics which makes a person recognizable by his voice alone. While two brothers in a close-knit family will begin to learn their language mainly from the same parents, they will inevitably have different speech experiences—as well as other experiences—in growing up; hence there will be differences, no matter how slight, in their speech habits. And even within the same person's speech, variations will occur according to situation, mood, educational experience, or whatever. In fact, a person never says the same word or sentence exactly the same way the second time, though the ear may not detect such slight differences.

So we may say that we extend from the individual with his idiolect to the community with its dialect to the nation with its language. The ideal language has been defined as a language spoken by just one person, in one frame of mind, at one time, in one place. But no such language or language speaker exists. Even given a hypothetical pair of speakers who for a particular moment spoke the same language exactly alike, by the time they had separated for a few days—maybe even less—they would come back together speaking the common language slightly differently. And next we come to some of the reasons languages change.

FOR FURTHER READING

Bolinger, Dwight, *Aspects of Language*, 2nd ed. New York: Harcourt Brace Jovanovich, 1975.

Dillard, J. L., *Black English*. New York: Random House, 1972.

The Florida FL Reporter, Vol. 5, No. 2 (Spring 1967); Vol. 6, No. 2 (Spring 1968).

Joos, Martin, *The Five Clocks*. New York: Harcourt Brace Jovanovich, 1967.

McDavid, Raven I., Jr., "The Dialects of American English," *The Structure of American English*, ed. W. Nelson Francis. New York: Ronald Press, 1958.

Malmstrom, Jean, and Annabel Ashley, *Dialects—USA*. Champaign, Ill.: NCTE, 1963.

Muller, Siegfried H., *The World's Living Languages*. New York: Frederick Ungar, 1964.

Partridge, Eric, *A Dictionary of Slang and Unconventional English*, 7th ed. New York: Macmillan, 1970.

Shores, David L., ed., *Contemporary English: Change and Variation.* Philadelphia: J. B. Lippincott, 1972.

Shuy, Roger W., ed., *Social Dialects and Language Learning.* Champaign, Ill.: NCTE, 1964.

Steiner, George, "A Future Literacy," *The Atlantic Monthly* (August 1971). Pp. 41–44.

Swadesh, Morris, *The Origin and Diversification of Language.* Chicago: Aldine Atherton, 1971.

There can never be a moment of true standstill in language, just as little as in the ceaselessly flaming thought of men.

Wilhelm von Humboldt

4

OLD LANGUAGES AND NEW

In Chapter 2, Jones and the Germanic "Big Three"—Rask, Bopp, and Grimm—were introduced, and mention was made of how they pioneered the COMPARATIVE METHOD of demonstrating relationships among different languages. Their work pretty well established the parent, or proto-Indo-European (PIE), language and its descendants. The astonishing thing is that such family relationships had not been worked out earlier. Most students today who speak English and one of the Italic languages would immediately notice a striking similarity in, say, "people," *peuple*, and *pueblo*. And even a monolingual English student would notice that Sanskrit *lih* closely resembles "lick," and *lok* is very like "look."

TABLE 4-1   Comparative Chart

English	Sanskrit	Latin	Greek	German	Old English	Old Norse	Gothic	Celtic
to bear	bhar	ferre	fero	gebären	beran	bera	baira	ber
father	pitar	pater	patir	Vater	fæder	faðir	fadar	aðir
mother	matar	mater	mitir	Mutter	modor	moðir	moþar	maðair
brother	bhratar	frater	frater	Bruder	broðor	broðir	broþar	braðair
three	trayas	tres	treis	drei	þrie	þre	þreis	tri
hundred	sata	centum	ekaton	hundert	hund	hundrað	hunda	ceað
night	nisitha	noctis	nikta	Nacht	niht	nott	nahts	
red	rudhira	ruber	erithros	rot	read	rjoðir	rauþs	
foot	pada	pedis	podos	Fuss	fot	fotr	fotus	
fish	piska	piscis	ikhthis	Fisch	fisc	fiskr	fisks	
goose	hamsa	anser	khin	Gans	gos	gas		
what	kwo	quod	ti	was	hwæt	hvat	hwas	
where	kva	quo	pou	wo	hwær	hvert		

Grimm's Law and Verner's Law

Of course, the obvious similarity of certain words in different languages had indeed been observed and recorded much earlier, but the linguists named above were the ones to begin a systematic study of such similarities and to derive rules for them, such as Grimm's law. The word "mother" is clearly related, or cognate, to the ancient Sanskrit *matar*, as well as to Latin *mater*, Greek *mitir*, German *Mutter*, Old English *modor*, Old Norse *moðir*.[1] Similarly, "three" in Sanskrit is *trayas*; in Latin, *tres*; in Greek, *treis*; in German, *drei*; in Old English, *þrie*; and in Old Norse, *þre*. The word "night" can also trace its relationship through Sanskrit *nisitha*, Latin *noctis*, Greek *nikta*, German *Nacht*, Old English *niht*, Old Norse *nott*. More imagination is needed to visualize the relationship in these words for "red": Sanskrit *rudhira* (actually, "blood"), Latin *ruber*, Greek *erithros*, German *rot*, Old English *read*, Old Norse *rjoðir*.

If we set up a chart and add more languages and vocabulary items (see Table 4-1), we can begin to reproduce the method used by the comparatists.

By gathering enormous quantities of existing language data, mainly from written records, the early comparative linguists determined kinship between languages by comparing cognate words, as in Table 4-1. They also codified the regular changes that took place within the individual languages by comparing each language with its earlier stages, as English students compare Old English with Middle English with Modern English. Thus a powerful tool was developed for reconstructing proto-languages for which no records were available, by reversing the order of these changes.

As more words were added to the lists, the regularity of certain phonetic, or sound, differences between words in

[1] Two characters that were used in Old English and Old Norse appear here: ð, called "eth," had the sound of "th" in "then"; þ, called "thorn," had the sound of "th" in "three."

related languages became obvious. It was observed, for example, that the word for "father" is quite similar in Sanskrit and many of the Western languages, but that the initial consonant in Sanskrit, Greek, and Latin is consistently /p/, while in the Germanic languages it is regularly /f/. The same CORRESPOND-ENCE of these initial sound-units is observable in such words as "fish": Latin *piscis*, German *Fisch*, Old English *fisc*; and "foot": Latin *pedis*, German *Fuss*, Old English *fot*. Where /p/ appears in non-Germanic, /f/ regularly occurs in the Germanic languages; thus, Germanic /f/ *corresponds* to non-Germanic /p/. Other correspondences are shown in Table 4-1.

Working independently, Rask (1818) and Grimm (1819) published their works demonstrating the regularity of the

TABLE 4-2

Grimm's Law

	Non-Germanic		*Germanic*		
Voiced aspirated stops[1] became (>) voiced stops:					
bh > b	Skt	bhratar	> ON	broðir	ModE brother
dh > d	Skt	rudhira	> OE	read	ModE red
gh > g	PIE	*ghosti[2]	> OE	gæst	ModE guest
Voiced stops became voiceless stops:					
b > p	L	cannabis	> ModE	hemp	
d > t	L	dentis	> OE	toð	ModE tooth
g > k	L	gens	> OE	cynn	ModE kin
Voiceless stops became voiceless spirants:					
p > f	Gr	podos	> OE	fot	ModE foot
t > θ[3]	Skt	trayas	> ON	þre	ModE three
k > h	L	centum	> OE	hund	ModE hundred

[1] This and other terms are explained in the Glossary and discussed in Chapter 5.
[2] The asterisk indicates a reconstructed form.
[3] The modern phonetic symbol for Old English "thorn" is θ.

SOUND-SHIFTS in cognate words in different Indo-European languages. These particular shifts in the Germanic languages occurred sometime during the first millennium B.C., after the various tribal movements had separated the Germanic peoples from the Roman and Greek tribes and other descendants of the proto-Indo-European language speakers.

The sets in Table 4-2 generally represent Grimm's law, showing the Germanic sound-shifts and the resulting correspondences between certain Germanic and non-Germanic consonants.

The sound-shifts within these sets occurred gradually, over hundreds of years. They were not continuing changes; once each change had occurred, it stopped.

FIGURE 4-1

How Consonants Changed

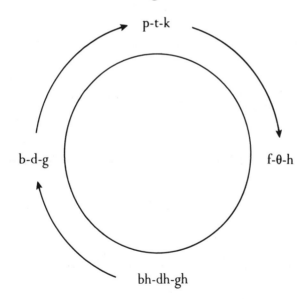

As Figure 4-1 shows, the wheel did not continue to spin, but made its quarter-turn and stopped.

As other linguists—or philologists—enthusiastically joined in the work of setting up comparative tables, more relationships were ascertained. Grimm's law worked beautifully in most cases, but did not allow for certain discrepancies that emerged from time to time. A glaring discrepancy was obvious in the word "hundred." According to Grimm's law, Latin *centum* should have developed into English *hunθred*. That is, Latin initial /k/ (the sound of *c* in *centum*) should have been English initial /h/—which it is—and Latin medial /t/ should have been English medial /θ/, a voiceless spirant, as in "*th*ink." But instead of the expected /θ/, we have /d/. It was not until 1877 that Karl Verner accounted for this and other exceptions. He showed that it was a matter of which syllable in a word got the heaviest stress in pronunciation. While early proto-Germanic had variable stress patterns similar to those of other Indo-European languages, later Germanic stress shifted mainly to the primary syllable, a characteristic apparent in English today. That is why we say "Máry," with the stress on the first syllable, while Romance languages, such as French and Italian, stress the final, *Maríe*, or the next to final, *María*. So, according to VERNER'S LAW, while the earlier form of Germanic "hundred" was undoubtedly **hunθred* (the asterisk indicates a reconstructed form not found in written documents), as the stress shifted from the final to the initial syllable, the voiceless spirant /θ/ gradually became the voiced stop /d/, the sound we hear today in "hundred."

The Indo-European Language

With the accounting for such exceptions to Grimm's law, Verner's law gave strength to the Neogrammarians' argument that sound-laws have no exception. This proven regularity allowed for RECONSTRUCTION of the proto-language, the parent language from which the Indo-European languages descended. The reconstruction method, put most simply, is to collect from the different but related languages as many words as possible which seem to have evolved from the same word, then surmise what the proto-word was. Take the word for "father." We know now that proto-Indo-European /p/ shifted to /f/ in the Germanic languages, so by restoring the initial /p/ to the corresponding words in the Germanic languages, we find that virtually all the languages attributed to the Indo-European family start their word for "father" with a /p/ (see Table 4-1). The medial consonant in the non-Germanic words for "father" is /t/, and since we know that according to Grimm's law the voiceless stop /t/ shifted to voiceless spirant /θ/ in the Germanic languages, we restore the original /t/ in all cases. Likewise, all the words for "father" seem to end in /r/. So as far as consonants are concerned, we can safely reconstruct the PIE word as *p-t-r*, the dashes standing for vowels. The vowel reconstruction calls for a bit more guesswork. On a majority count, most of the words for "father" have the first vowel represented as /a/. However, we must not be misled by the spelling, since spelling is only the approximate representation of the way the words were actually pronounced. Also, the first syllable—except in later Germanic—was the unstressed syllable; hence in actual pronunciation the first vowel could have varied from unstressed /ə/ (the initial vowel in "suppose") to a more open /a/ or even to /i/ (the relaxed vowel sound in "milk"). The last syllable was stressed; therefore, the vowel in that syllable was certainly more distinct. It could have been /a/ or it could have been /ɛ/ (the vowel sound in "met"), or less likely, even something else.

Syllabic stress was variable in PIE. In fact, this variation in stress is generally supposed to have been at least partially the cause of ABLAUT in the Indo-European family of languages. Ablaut is a regular alternation of vowels in a root, or the basic part of a word, indicating a grammatical change, such as tense. In English it is most apparent in the irregular verbs, such as: "swim," "swam," "swum"; "ride," "rode," "ridden"; "sing," "sang," "sung." Modern English has eliminated much of this ablaut by regularizing many of the verbs which were irregular in Old English. For example:

Old English	Modern English
gielt, geald, golden	yield, yielded, yielded
birst, bærst, borsten	burst, burst, burst
hilpþ, healp, holpen	help, helped, helped

Before discussing the comparative method of reconstruction further, it would be well to review some other factors besides phonetic correspondences which support the hypothesis for a proto-Indo-European language. A primary factor would be the similarity of what we may call BASIC VOCABULARY in the Indo-European languages—that is, words for numbers, parts of the body, family relationships, natural phenomena such as sun, moon, stars, and so on. These words have been shown to be least susceptible to change. Reconstructed PIE has a large inventory of such vocabulary items. Significantly, reconstructed PIE has no word for "iron," since that metal was discovered after PIE had dispersed into several different languages.

These proto-Indo-European ancestors did have a word for "wheel," for "axle," and others signifying wheeled means of transportation. They had words for "pig," "barley," "plowing," "settlement," and "pasture," suggesting that they were an agricultural rather than a nomadic people, hence restricted to a relatively small geographic area. No words have been reconstructed for "palm tree," "vine," "rice," "monkey," and "crocodile." By inference from this negative evidence, we can suppose that Asia and Africa and the Mediterranean countries were not the original homeland.

On the other hand, the proto-Indo-Europeans had words for such trees as "birch," "beech," "oak," and others which are native to a more northerly temperate climate. "Bear," "wolf," and "deer" also indicate such a climate, as does "snow." Another key word present in most of the Indo-European languages is *laks* ("salmon"), bearing a close resemblance to the modern German word *Lachs*. While the southerly migrating tribes such as the Italic and Greek found no salmon in their new homelands, and as a matter of course soon lost the word, the term remains in recognizable form in the more northerly language families.

With these and numerous other terms and characteristics to infer from, the majority of linguistic scholars center the homeland of the proto-Indo-Europeans in the northern part of middle Europe, probably in the area of Poland and East Germany. Sometime between 3000 and 4000 B.C. (the hypothesis goes) these people began several waves of migrations that carried them as far as the Scandinavian countries to the west, and to India in the east. They were powerful and established themselves as the rulers in the areas they settled; thus their language remained the predominant one.

For a while the comparatists believed that Sanskrit itself was the proto-language of the Indo-European family, but that idea was soon abandoned. Sanskrit has remained—so far—the oldest Indo-European language recorded, although the decipherment of Linear B tablets (discussed in Chapter 11) may perhaps establish Mycenaean Greek as the oldest Indo-European language recorded. Modern historical linguists still consider that Sanskrit, with its highly developed inflectional system, must resemble the proto-language rather closely.

August Schleicher (whom we discussed in Chapter 2) broke the practice of citing Sanskrit as PIE, and introduced the asterisked form for reconstructed words in PIE. He also introduced the STAMMBAUM, or family tree model, to illustrate the Indo-European language relationships. For clarity, if not for complete accuracy, this model, now modified, is still widely used. A representational model is shown in Figure 4-2.

Although there is little doubt now about the previous existence of the PIE language, the classification and relationships of the daughter families cannot be considered exact. Figure 4-2 shows ten subfamilies, but does not give all the languages in those subfamilies. Some scholars name only nine subfamilies.

FIGURE 4-2

Indo-European Language Family Tree

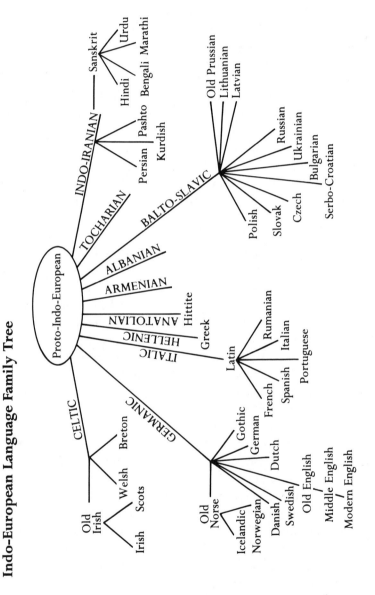

And we must remember that entire subfamilies may have completely vanished in the mists of the past. Tocharian, a language long forgotten, was only rediscovered in the twentieth century, as was Hittite. Work is still being carried on in PIE reconstruction and in the classification of Indo-European languages.

It was suggested above that the tree schema does not show precisely the development of hundreds of families from a proto-language. Figure 4-2 suggests that a clean splitting away from an original language occurred. This is not true. There was a period when the ancestors of the recorded languages were in contact, but they gradually, probably *very* gradually, developed dialectal differences that became more and more pronounced as groups and tribes began to lose contact with each other. A dialectal continuum, not a sharply defined family tree, best describes the linguistic relationships among the Indo-European stock at this early period.

In 1872, Johannes Schmidt proposed his WAVE theory of the breakup of the proto-language. Starting from the observation that correspondences can be found between any two branches of Indo-European, but that those branches lying closest to each other have the highest percentage of correspondences, he suggested that languages move out and overlap each other in waves. The second wave from the proto-fountain may carry certain speech changes not included in the earlier wave, and may move over an area not covered by the first wave. Successive waves, reflecting the inevitable changes inherent in any language, will develop in still other areas. Figure 4-3 illustrates the wave theory.

An example of such overlappings and internal changes would be the French speech which went into England by way of the Norman invasions from 1066, and the French speech which went into Vietnam from the end of the eighteenth century. The Old French word *chaiere* came into English with something like the Modern English pronunciation "chair." However, in France during the thirteenth and fourteenth centuries, the initial sound changed from *ch* to *sh*, although the spelling remained practically the same. And so the Vietnamese were given Modern French *chaire* and *chaise*, pronounced like "share" and "shez." In part, then, the wave theory accounts for the distinct characteristics of Canadian and Louisiana French, as compared with Modern Parisian French. However, other forces are involved, too.

FIGURE 4-3

The Wave Theory

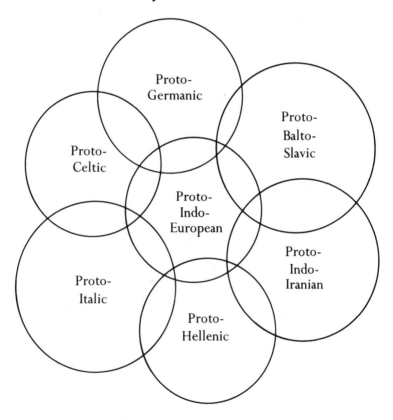

A danger exists in trying to relate languages strictly through words that are mainly nominals, that is, nouns or words used as nouns. BORROWING accounts for the appearance of many cognate words in two languages, and sheer coincidence accounts for others. As a result of our relations with Japan, both peaceful and warlike, Americans have borrowed and adopted such words as *tsunami*, *zori*, *zabuton*, *bonsai*, and *kamikaze*. The Japanese have returned the favor by adopting *date*, *cocktail*, *table*, *toilet*, and others. Yet we know that English and Japanese are not descendants of a common proto-language. The British word "hanger" for a type of sword was adopted probably as early as the Crusades from the Arabic word *khanjar*. The Spanish exclamation *Ojala!* which translates into something like "Oh, how I hope!" is from the Arabic exclamation *O Allah!* but evidence indicates that neither English nor Spanish is related to Arabic by linguistic ancestry.

HOMONYMS (Greek *homonumos* = "same name") are words that sound alike and look alike, but have different meanings. Many homonyms exist among unrelated languages. *Torah* in Hebrew means "instruction, law"; *tora* in Greek means "now"; and *tora* in Japanese means "tiger." This phenomenon is merely coincidence, as is the fact that Japanese *tori* means "way," a meaning which could be strained to fit the Hebrew meaning of *torah*. Japanese *onna* and Italian *donna* both mean "woman"; German *Buch* and Quiché *buj* both mean "book"; Greek *mati* and Malay *mata* both mean "eye." Such FALSE COGNATES, or chance similarities, may run as high as 4 percent between languages without attested kinship. Margaret Schlauch has commented that words that look like words in other languages are probably unrelated for that very reason: because of regular sound-shifts and other phenomena, a word will change in structure and even in meaning in a relatively short time.

We have observed how false cognates may occur through the law of probability, or simply through the borrowing of words from one language into another. As Rask pointed out over a century and a half ago, a far more certain indication of relationship between languages is in grammatical agreement. Grammatical forms, for instance, are seldom borrowed back and forth, and thus are truer indications of the original language. The following table indicates such grammatical relationships among certain Indo-European languages:

	Modern English	Old English	Sanskrit	Latin	Greek
Singular	I am	ic eom	asmi	sum	eimi
	you are	þu eart	asi	es	ei
	he is	he is	asti	est	esti
Plural	we are	we sindon	smas	sumus	esmen
	you are	ge sindon	stha	estis	este
	they are	hie sindon	santi	sunt	eisi

Some differences inevitably exist between the old and new forms in any language. The following brief paradigm, or model, of the verb "to love," compares Latin and one of its new forms, Modern French:

	Latin	French
Singular	*amo*	*aime*
	amas	*aimes*
	amat	*aime*
Plural	*amamus*	*aimons*
	amatis	*aimez*
	amant	*aiment*

Since Modern French is not spelled phonetically, the sharp distinctions in pronunciation of the two forms is not apparent from the spelling.

How Languages Change

How and why did the several daughter languages become so different from the parent language, and so different from one another? According to linguist Sven Liljeblad, the lifetime of a language as it is spoken at a certain time can be no longer than approximately eight hundred years. The modern Greek student must study classical Greek as a foreign language, just as today's French student must learn early medieval French, or an English student King Alfred's Anglo-Saxon.

A major reason for language change is, to borrow Sapir's term, DRIFT. There exist dynamics, or forces, so consistent as to be called inherent factors in language itself, which cause language to gradually change. One such factor, called by Morris Halle "discontinuities in the grammars of successive generations," indicates by its label that changes take place to a certain degree in speech patterns from one generation to the next. While the preschool child patterns his speech after his parents' speech, as he grows older he is influenced far more by the speech of his peers. Yet drift is very gradual, even unnoticeable, so that no generation of native speakers is actually aware that it is changing any of the forms of the language. The Old English pronunciations of *ban* and *stan* developed over centuries into "bone" and "stone."

Another factor which might be subsumed under drift is conservation of energy—or ECONOMY, as the French linguist André Martinet expresses it. This is the tendency to choose an easier form of a linguistic unit and gradually phase out the more difficult. An example of economy would be the erosion of the initial *h* in many Old English words as they moved gradually toward Modern English. The Anglo-Saxon said *hlaf* for "loaf," and *hring* for "ring," and *hit* for "it." You may judge for yourself how much more effort is required to pronounce the older forms. The Anglo-Saxon also said *hwæt* for "what," an interrogative pronounced the same as "watt" in parts of the English-speaking world today. In these same dialectal regions the interrogative "which" is pronounced "witch." A current word, "cupboard," reveals its original pronunciation by its antiquated spelling; but today it is reduced in pronunciation to "cubberd."

Another phonetic, or sound, change somewhat akin to economy is ASSIMILATION, the process by which a sound changes to more closely resemble a neighboring sound. The operative force in this case is ENVIRONMENT, or the effect of one sound on an adjacent one. A child says "grampa" instead of "grandpa," choosing the path of least effort. He collapses the consonant cluster /ndp/ and joins the /p/ to the preceding /m/ because both /p/ and /m/ are formed in the same way, with the lips pressed together. The same force is operative when the airline announcer says "emplane" rather than "enplane." The Arab speaker, in prefixing a noun with *al* ("the"), will in certain cases assimilate the final *l* of *al* to the first sound of the noun. *Al-salaam alaykum*, the greeting of "the peace be upon you," is pronounced *as-salaam alaykum*. Likewise, *al-shams* ("the sun") is pronounced *ash-shams*, and *al-rajul* ("the man") is pronounced *ar-rajul*. The spelling in Arabic, however, continues to show the *l*. Assimilation can even produce an erroneous interpretation and ultimately a different word. In an Algonquian dialect, the expression *missi wabu*, which meant something like "the great light of the dawn," became assimilated to *missabo*, a word which meant "rabbit." Gradually, then, the two meanings merged into a mythical personification of the dawn as a large rabbit.

The influence of environment was responsible for the Germanic sound-change known as I-UMLAUT, a form of assimilation which occurred mainly sometime before the seventh century A.D. You may demonstrate this change for yourself by pronouncing aloud the illustrations in this paragraph. First, pronounce "foot" and then "feet." Notice that the vowel sound of "foot" is formed low in the mouth, but the vowel sound of "feet" is produced high in the front of the mouth. Now, early Old English had *fot* (rhymes with "float") for "foot," and **fotiz* for the plural form. The early speaker, anticipating the /i/ ("ee") sound in the second syllable of **fotiz*, shaped his speech organs for that sound, thus causing the first vowel, /o/, to approximate the sound of /i/. Gradually two forms resulted: singular *fot* and plural **fetiz*. Since Germanic stress is on the primary syllable, the final /iz/ of the plural form eventually eroded, leaving the two forms *fot* and *fet*. This was also a case of linguistic economy, for since the two basic syllables were now distinct—singular and plural—there was no longer any need for the plural inflectional ending /iz/. That the i-umlaut change is still sometimes in effect may be attested by the modern pronunciation of "pretty" ("pritty"), in which the first vowel anticipates the final "y."

Still another type of linguistic change is METATHESIS, the transposing of sounds within a word. In English, "bird" used to be *bridd*; "thresh" was *þerscan*; "ask" was both *æcs* and *æsc*; "bright" was *beorht*; "through" was *thurgh*. Spanish *palabra* ("word") is a transposition of Late Latin *parabola* ("speech"). Apparently, metathesis occurs in all languages. Bloomfield noted examples of it in Tagalog, a non-Indo-European language.

A Look at the English Language

It seems, then, that language change and its causes can be divided into two broad classes: change resulting from the inherent nature of language; and change resulting from external contacts, such as war and trade. Both types of change may be illustrated by a few highlights in the history of English. Like PIE, Old English was a highly inflected language. Nouns had five cases, each case distinguished mainly by its inflectional endings— much like Latin. Nearly half of the OE nouns were inflected as follows:

Nominative	se cyning	the king
Genitive	þæs cyninges	of the king
Dative	þæm cyninge	to the king
Accusative	þone cyning	the king
Instrumental	þy cyning	by the king

During the tenth and eleventh centuries England was invaded by Viking raiders who spoke a Germanic dialect similar enough to Old English to be understandable to the Anglo-Saxons. The invaders became settlers, and communication between the two peoples caused changes in Old English.

Although the Viking and the Anglo-Saxon dialects were close, variations existed in both inflectional endings and vocabulary items. The majority of the people were illiterate, so they carried no visual images of the words in their minds; pronunciation was controlled by the ear only. Since the word-root (like *cyning*, on p. 75), with its Germanic stress, carried the bulk of the meaning, the pronunciation of the nonstressed endings were gradually mumbled away. Word order, plus an increased use of prepositions, articles, and other grammatical particles, filled the function of grammatical meaning. Thus, phonetic changes will sometimes result in grammatical and other changes. Today, the plural ''-s'' and the genitive '''s'' are all that remain of noun inflections. (However, scholars now recognize that this inflectional erosion was occurring even before the invasions.)

One pronunciation did not replace another in every case. *Scyrte*, the Anglo-Saxon ''shirt,'' was pronounced much as it is today. It collided with the Viking *skyrta*. Instead of one word replacing the other, both were retained, but with separate meanings, yielding Modern English ''shirt'' and ''skirt.'' This explains why we have such pairs as ''shrub'' and ''scrub,'' ''shriek'' and ''screech,'' ''dish'' and ''disk.''

The Norman Conquest of 1066 caused further tremendous changes in the English language by superimposing Norman French on the native Anglo-Saxon speech. Not only did the vocabulary change, but word-order and grammatical changes were so severe that Middle English—as the language after about 1100 is called—is actually a different language from Old English. However, the grammatical changes were not entirely a result of contact with the French language; decay of inflections and other grammatical changes were speeded up through the conditions brought on by the Conquest itself, such as the wholesale slaughter of the educated class of Anglo-Saxons.

A brief example from Anglo-Saxon and from Middle English will illustrate the sharp distinctions between the two:

Old English

Dæghwamlice man unriht rærde ealles to wide gynd ealle þas þeode.
(Every day they have committed injustice all too widely in all this nation.)

Middle English

This carpenter hadde wedded newe a wyf,
Which that he lovede moore than his lyf.

The second example hardly needs a translation.

One of the greatest phonetic changes occurred in English over a relatively short period of time, from the time of Chaucer to the time of Shakespeare, roughly two centuries. This set of changes is called, aptly enough, the GREAT VOWEL SHIFT. Old English had long vowels as well as short vowels, the distinction being in length of stress—that is, how long the vowel was sounded. For example, *hran* means "whale," but *hrān* (with the *a* held longer) means "reindeer." Many of these long vowels carried over into Middle English, and it was on them that the change took place. The effect was a raising of each vowel to the next level of formation in the mouth, except for the two vowels which were already as high as they could go. These two developed into DIPHTHONGS, the double sounds of "oy" in "boy" and "ow" in "howl." The change is shown in Figure 4-4.

Just exactly why this vowel shift took place is not known. Probably the change was so gradual that no single generation noticed it. Once the process began, though, many words which had been pronounced differently before began to sound confusingly alike. The word for "greet" was pronounced "great" in Middle English. The word for "late" was pronounced "let." So, unconsciously perhaps, the speakers of the fourteenth and fifteenth centuries continued to shift the vowels in order to re-establish the equilibrium of the language, to make it clearer.

We have already referred to borrowing as a language change

FIGURE 4-4

The Great Vowel Shift[1]

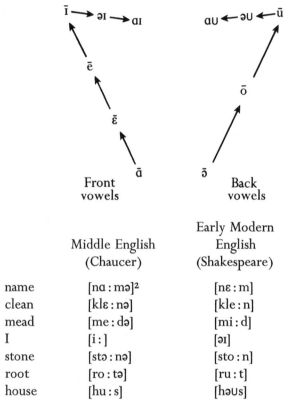

	Middle English (Chaucer)	Early Modern English (Shakespeare)
name	[nɑ : mə][2]	[nɛ : m]
clean	[klɛ : nə]	[kle : n]
mead	[me : də]	[mi : d]
I	[i :]	[əɪ]
stone	[stɔ : nə]	[sto : n]
root	[ro : tə]	[ru : t]
house	[hu : s]	[həUs]

[1] Table 5-1 gives the equivalents of the phonetic characters, which are enclosed in brackets.

[2] The colon [:], like the overmark [¯], indicates a long vowel, to be held a bit in pronunciation.

resulting from the external contacts of war, trade, tourism, and the like. When a word is borrowed from another language, a pronunciation change generally occurs, since the phonetic inventory of the culture borrowing the word is rarely similar to that of the culture borrowed from. The change may result from substitution of native speech-sounds for the nonnative ones. Or it may result from addition of sounds, or even subtraction of sounds in the original word or phrase. For example, the Hawaiian language has no *r* and no *s*. Consequently, when the Hawaiians adopted the English expression "Merry Christmas," it came out as *Mele Kalikimaka*. Similarly, the Pueblo Indians and the Navajos in the Southwest call Albuquerque *Vokeki*, which is a rendering of the sound as they hear it, reproduced in the speech-sounds available to them in their own languages. Words which the Japanese took from Americans have become reshaped to such an extent that often they are unrecognizable to Americans. "Touring" has become *tsuringu*, "violin" is *waiorin*, "process" is *purosesu*, "type" is *taipu*, "table" is *taboru*, "baseball" is *beisaboru*, "cocktail" is *kakuteiru*. The same adaptation process occurs when Americans borrow from other languages. The native Frenchman clenches his teeth in visible torment when he hears "lonjeray" for *lingerie*, or "shayz-lounge" for *chaise-longue*. Americans have also transmuted many Spanish terms, including "buckaroo" for *vaquero*, "hoosegow" for *juzgado*, "calaboose" for *calabozo*, and "lariat" for *la reata*. Thousands of such examples of borrowing may be observed by scanning a good dictionary and noting the etymology of the various terms.

Upon the impressive groundwork laid by the Neogrammarians, and with the continuing collection of data and the refinement of methodology, the task of reconstruction of languages continues. Just as the ultimate goal of the astronauts in collecting and analyzing materials and data from the moon is to produce such a highly refined model of lunar evolution that, by extended calculation, the genesis of the solar system may be inferred, so the aim of linguists is to assemble models of current languages and, by extension, to create models of proto-languages.

Language Studies Today

The Indo-European language family remains the most completely described today, but that does not mean it will

TABLE 4-3

Primitive Central Algonquian

	Fox	Ojibwa	Menomini	Cree	*PCA [1]
He is old.	kehkjɛ:wa		kɛčki:w		kečkjɛ:wa
fire	aškutɛ:wi	iškudɛ:	esko:tɛ:w	iskute:w	iškutɛ:wi
moccasin	mahkesɛ:hi	mahkizin	mahkɛ:sen	maskisin	maxkesini
my grandmother	no:hkumesa	no:hkumis	no:hkumɛh	no:hkum	no:hkuma
He kicks him.	takeškawɛ:wa	tangiškawa:d	tahkɛ:skawɛ:w	tahkiskawɛ:w	tankeškawɛ:wa

[1] The words in this column are reconstructed forms of Primitive Central Algonquian.

continue to be so. By the first decade of the twentieth century, Leonard Bloomfield had already applied the comparative method of reconstruction to three Pacific languages: Tagalog, Javanese, Batak—and produced through correspondences a set of Primitive Indonesian forms. With commendable scientific restraint, Bloomfield cautioned against taking these reconstructed forms as truly representative of the earlier terms; they were more or less accurate approximations. More recent linguists working in the Malayo-Polynesian languages, an extremely complex linguistic group, have applied the comparative and reconstructive methods to attest the kinship of hundreds of diverse languages.

Bloomfield also reconstructed a set of Primitive (or proto-) Central Algonquian forms, using data from four living languages of related Indian tribes: Fox, Ojibwa, Menomini, and Cree. A look at Table 4-3 will reveal the similarities in the items which convinced Bloomfield of their kinship.

Even before Bloomfield, anthropologists were attempting to count and classify the North American Indian languages. In 1891, an official bulletin classified over two hundred North American tribes into fifty-eight language groups. In 1929, Sapir reduced these fifty-eight groups to six groups, beyond which he could see no further relationships. Today, the Bureau of Indian Affairs accepts eight major linguistic families: Algonquian, Iroquois, Caddo, Muskhogean, Siouan, Penutian, Athapascan, and Uto-Aztecan. (Some linguists still do not accept such a reduction in numbers of separate families, while at least one— Morris Swadesh—has suggested that all the Indian languages come from one common ancestor.) An interested student has only to pick up a current copy of the *International Journal of American Linguistics* to see the tremendous amount of work going on in analysis and classification of the Indian languages.

While kinship has been attested and reconstruction has been made possible through the comparative method, the method does not often indicate *when* linguistic changes occurred. In the early 1950s, Morris Swadesh and other linguists attempted to develop a tool to measure just when the daughter languages "split away" from the parent language, or when certain linguistic changes occurred. This tool, known as GLOTTOCHRONOLOGY, or LEXICOSTATISTICS, may be defined as the study of rate of change in language. Its application is based upon a principle stated early in the century by Sapir: "The greater the degree of linguistic differentiation within a stock the greater is the period of time that must be assumed for the development of such differentiation." A further principle is the implication within the Neogrammarians' axiom that speech-sounds change according to absolute laws—therefore, they change at a regular rate.

Using Dr. Willard Libby's carbon-14 dating process as a model for analogy, Swadesh and others worked with languages whose times of separation were known, such as English and German, and developed the formula

$$t = \frac{\log C}{2 \log r}$$

in which t equals the time in years, r equals the rate of retention of basic vocabulary per thousand years, and C equals the percentage of cognates found between two test lists. Using known languages, it was found that r is approximately 80 or 81 percent per thousand years. That is, two languages separating will each retain 81 percent of their original basic vocabulary at the end of a thousand years, but not the same 81 percent. At the end of the second thousand years, they will retain 81 percent of the first 81 percent, and so on. So, if two related languages are found with 66 percent (81 percent of 81 percent) cognate items in basic vocabulary, we assume that they separated approximately a thousand years ago (see Figure 4-5).

Recognizing that vocabulary as a whole cannot be counted on for regularity—language is affected by cultural borrowing and other irregular influences of change—linguists interested in the glottochronological, or lexicostatistical, method developed a set of terms that seem basic to all cultures, therefore least subject to abrupt change (see p. 66). These basic words include terms for parts of the body, kinship, natural phenomena; verbs such as "go," "come," "eat," "drink"; and adjectives such as "old," "new," "big," "small."

At this time the application of the glottochronological tool has produced some fairly spectacular results, but it has also been severely criticized and completely rejected by a number of reputable linguists. A major problem is that the "basic" terms are

FIGURE 4-5

Language-Dating Diagram

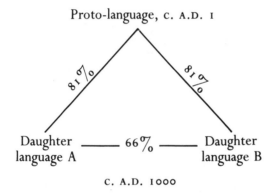

Proto-language, c. A.D. I

81% 81%

Daughter language A ——— 66% ——— Daughter language B

C. A.D. 1000

not necessarily basic from culture to culture. There is also serious doubt that the rate of vocabulary retention is constant from language to language. Nevertheless, it would seem that with some mathematical refinement, the tool may still be used—if not as an exact dating device, at least as a practical tool for approximate dating.

FOR FURTHER READING

Arlotto, Anthony, *Introduction to Historical Linguistics*. Boston: Houghton Mifflin, 1972.

Baugh, Albert C., *A History of the English Language*, 2nd ed. New York: Appleton-Century-Crofts, 1957.

Gordon, James O., *The English Language: A Historical Introduction*. New York: Thomas Y. Crowell, 1972.

Hymes, D. H., "Lexicostatistics So Far," *Current Anthropology*, Vol. 1 (January 1960). Pp. 3–44.

Laird, Charlton, and Robert M. Gorrell, eds., *Reading About Language*. New York: Harcourt Brace Jovanovich, 1971.

Lehmann, Winfred P., *Historical Linguistics: An Introduction*. New York: Holt, Rinehart and Winston, 1962.

Pyles, Thomas, *The Origin and Development of the English Language*, 2nd ed. New York: Harcourt Brace Jovanovich, 1971.

Thieme, Paul, "The Indo-European Language," *Scientific American* (October 1958). Pp. 63–74.

Watkins, Calvert, "Appendix: Indo-European and the Indo-Europeans," *The American Heritage Dictionary of the English Language*. Boston: Houghton Mifflin, 1969.

II

LANGUAGE: STRUCTURE AND MEANING

The difference between distinctive and non-distinctive features of sound lies entirely in the habit of the speakers.

Leonard Bloomfield

5

PHONOLOGY

When linguists speak of language, unless they specify otherwise they are discussing *spoken* language. Spoken language is a system of vocal symbols, or speech-sounds. The study of how these symbols, or sounds, are produced and used is PHONOLOGY, which includes phonetics and phonemics. The distinction between these two terms will become clear in the following pages.

Languages and Sounds

The beginner in linguistics, as well as the layman, is often confused or irritated upon first encountering a transcription such as this:

/ðə kugɚ krautʃt ɪn ðə bauz ovɚhɛd/

Why not write it simply as this?

The cougar crouched in the boughs overhead.

A moment's reflection gives the answer: the English alphabet—and many others, for that matter—does not accurately and regularly record the speech-sounds made by a speaker. George Bernard Shaw's joking example makes the point quite clear. He demonstrated that from a phonetic standpoint, "fish" may just as reasonably be spelled "ghoti." His argument: the final sound in "enou*gh*" is "f"; the sound of the first vowel in "w*o*men" is "i"; the sound of the middle letters in "na*ti*on" is "sh." In English, examples of sound and letter not matching may be multiplied almost without end.

Similarly, in standard Spanish the written letter *h* is not pronounced in *hoy, hijo, hielo,* and other words. However, the written letter *j* is pronounced as "h" in words such as *Juan, jíbaro, joven.* In German, *v* is pronounced as "f": *Vater, Volk, verloben,* while *w* is pronounced as "v": *Wagen, wie, wissen.* Other languages present still other examples of apparent inconsistency between the written representation of a speech-sound and its actual formation. In Greek, the sound "ee" may be represented by six written symbols: *H, I, Y, EI, OI, YI;* they're all pronounced alike.

During the last century the International Phonetic Association realized the impossibility of doing transcription work without a standard system of notation, so in 1888 the International Phonetic Alphabet (IPA) was developed. Based mainly on the Latin alphabet, it was subject to modifications almost from the start, to accommodate sounds which did not correspond to the limited number of sounds symbolized by the Latin letters. While virtually every language in the world is restricted to an inventory of fifteen to fifty meaningful sound-units (phonemes), the total number of sound-units of all the languages goes into the hundreds. Nor is the human speech apparatus restricted to these hundreds; there is an indefinitely large number of sounds that could conceivably be used for communication. However, every language has a tendency toward economy, a tendency that restricts its inventory of speech-sounds rather than multiplying them (see p. 73). As languages pick up new sounds, they also drop old sounds which no longer seem necessary. English used to have long vowels, as does classical Latin. In Old English, the words for "good" and "God" were spelled alike and pronounced alike, except that in speech *gōd* ("good") was pronounced with a longer *o* than *god* ("God"). That is, the vowel sound was held longer. We no longer depend upon distinctions of vowel length for different meanings.

Before the development of the IPA—and linguistic training—many people, mainly travelers, had written down unknown languages as they *thought* they heard them pronounced by native speakers. While some had better ears than others, they still wrote in the alphabet which they were accustomed to. One has only to look through early American historical records to see how John Smith and others interpreted the sound-signals of Indian words, or how newcomers to Hawaii spelled Polynesian words. Puritan John Winthrop's journal spells "sassafras" as *saxafras*. Captain Cook called the island of Oahu, *Wouahoo*, and Hawaii was *Owhyhee*, while Captain Vancouver called King Kamehameha *Tamaahmaah*. Herman Melville's New England speech habits got in his way: he spelled "koa wood" *koar-wood*. A rugged individuality is obvious.

Even today one of the hardest things for a person learning another language is to become accustomed to the fact that the target language does not employ the precise speech-sounds of his own language. The Frenchman studying English must learn to pronounce "th," a sound not used in French; the German must learn the double consonant "wh," as in "what"; the Spaniard must distinguish between "seat" and "sit"; the Japanese must distinguish between "cloud" and "crowd." The American studying Chinese must learn to hear and to pronounce retroflex *hs*. If learning Navajo, he must master voiceless *ł*; if he is learning Parisian French, he has to struggle with uvular *r*. These sounds and many others do not occur in American English. Of course, another problem for the second-language learner is that unless he has had some sort of special training in speech, he is usually quite vague about how he shapes his own native speech sounds; his native language is more of an unconscious habit than it is a conscious effort.

The purpose, then, of the IPA is to present a visual symbol of every speech-sound as it is used in its native language. As more and more of the so-called exotic languages are being transcribed, it becomes necessary from time to time for the field linguist to make modifications or additions to his list of symbols to accommodate those sounds in the target language not accounted for by his ready inventory. The invention of the portable tape recorder has been a tremendous asset to the field worker, but only a little experience in the field will reveal its shortcomings. One weakness is that no tape recorder can match in fidelity the eye and ear of a trained linguist; the linguist is able to watch the movements of the lips and sometimes the tongue, pinpointing the location of formation of each sound, and thus distinguish between two sounds which may sound quite similar in a playback from the tape. Field notes plus the tape recording work beautifully together.

A laboratory device is the SPECTROGRAPH, which visually records the sound waves of speech, clearly categorizing the separate speech-sounds as to frequency (the number of sound waves per second produced by a particular sound). Other technical devices can measure even more precisely the phonetic units of speech, making these aspects of linguistics more and more an exact science. Such data and such devices are of tremendous value in analysis of speech production.

The speech-sound which we have been referring to may be either a PHONE or a PHONEME. The phone is the speech-sound as it is actually made, and falls under PHONETICS; the phoneme is the speech-sound as it is interpreted by the hearer, and falls under PHONEMICS. We will consider phonetics first. Again, phonetics is concerned with the precise sound as it is made, the position and movement of the tongue and lips, the tension and vibration of the sound-making vocal cords, the force of the aspiration of breath from the lungs. Brackets—[ ]—are used to enclose phonetic notations, and slashes—/ /—are used to enclose phonemic transcriptions. Phonetic transcriptions are more refined, or precise, than phonemic ones.

How Sounds Are Made

In order to understand the phonological description which follows, it will be necessary to look at Figure 5-1, an illustration of the speech-making apparatus, and to learn the terms given there. Now, what happens when we form phones and string them together to create speech?

Basically, the lungs force air up the windpipe through the larynx, or voice box, which contains the vocal cords. The cords, which are two elastic bands of muscle, may be lax or tense, and the tension determines how high or how low the sound will be, just like the tension in the strings of a violin or guitar. The sound-units are further shaped in the pharynx, or the pharyngeal passage. The muscles which are used for swallowing food can also be used to enlarge or narrow the passage, thus altering the sound. As we shall see, some languages use the pharyngeal muscles more than other languages do. The greatest modification of the phone takes place in the mouth, mainly by raising, lowering, or otherwise flexing the tongue. Figure 5-2 shows how the tongue plays its part in forming some of the phones of the vowel spectrum.

So we see that the position of the tongue in the mouth is the main controlling factor in the formation of vowels, and for this reason we speak of vowels as "high," "low," "front," "back," "mid," or any combination of these. The initial vowel in "upon" is a mid-vowel; the vowel in "feet" is a high front vowel; and the vowel in "cough" is a low back vowel. Of course, the shape of the lips also plays a part, as you can readily see by looking in a mirror while forming the vowels.

FIGURE 5-1

The Speech-Making Apparatus

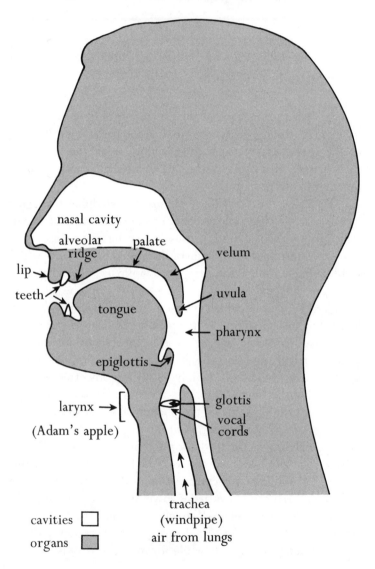

FIGURE 5-2

The Formation of Vowels[1]

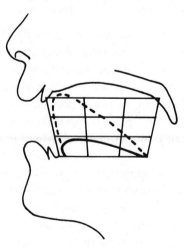

High

i		y		u
				U
ɪ		ɨ		
e	ø			o
		ə		
ɛ				
æ				
		a		ɔ
				ɑ

Front   Back

Low

[1] The symbols in this chart do not represent all the vowel sounds of the world's languages. Also, the positions are only approximate, varying from language to language, and from dialect to dialect.

Broken line = tongue position for "feet"
Solid line = tongue position for "fat"

Table 5-1 gives the pronunciation of the vowels in Figure 5-2.

TABLE 5-1

The Pronunciation of Vowels

[i]	feet (American)	[ɔ]	thought (Am)
[ɪ]	fit (Am)	[o]	soap (Am)
[e]	late (Am)	[u]	boot (Am)
[ɛ]	let (Am)	[ʊ]	put (Am)
[ø]	feu (French)	[y]	Hütte (German)
[æ]	sat (Am)	[ɨ]	milk (Am)
[a]	casa (Spanish)	[ə]	upon (Am)
[ɑ]	father (Am)		

DIPHTHONGS, a blending of two vowels by a sort of glide, are generally symbolized in American English as follows:

[ei]	play	[ɔi]	toy
[ɑi]	buy	[ɑʊ]	cow

Phones, or speech-sounds, are broadly classified into two groups, STOPS and CONTINUANTS, depending upon whether the flow of air is shut off with the sound-formation, or whether the flow continues. All vowels are continuants; that is, any vowel can be sounded as long as the breath holds out. On the other hand, a consonant like "p" is stopped the moment it is sounded. The stoppage of air flow may occur anywhere along the sound tract from the glottis to the lips. Consonants are distinguished from vowels by either a complete stoppage of air, or by some degree of obstruction of the passage of air somewhere in the vocal tract.

Consonants are classified by the positions at which they are formed, or points of articulation (see Table 5-2). The best way to relate the following terms to their positions is to study Figure 5-1 and Tables 5-2 and 5-3, and to practice the sounds while looking in a mirror. A BILABIAL is a consonant formed by putting the upper and lower lips together. Examples of bilabial consonants are [p], [b], [m]. A LABIODENTAL is a consonant formed by

TABLE 5-2   The Classification of Consonants[1]

	Bilabial	Labio-dental	Dental	Alveolar	Palatal	Velar	Uvular	Glottal	Pharyn-geal
Stops vl[2]	p			t tʃ		k q		ʔ	
vd	b			d dʒ		g			
Fricatives vl		f	θ	s	ç ʃ	x		h	H
(or spirants) vd	β	v	ð	z	ʒ	ɣ			
Nasals	m			n	ɲ	ŋ			
Liquids vl				ɬ					
vd				R r l			R		
Glides	w				ʎ j				

[1] This chart is not complete, but serves only to show the approximate positions of some of the more common consonants.

[2] "Vl" stands for "voiceless," "vd" for "voiced."

touching the upper teeth against the lower lip, like [f], [v]. A
DENTAL is formed with the tip of the tongue against the upper
teeth, like [θ], [ð]. An ALVEOLAR is formed with the tip of the
tongue against the alveolar ridge, like [t], [d]. A PALATAL is
formed with the tongue against the palate, like [ʃ], [ʒ], [ʎ]. A
VELAR is formed with the tongue against the velum, like [k],
[g]. A UVULAR is formed with the back of the tongue vibrating
against the uvula, like the French and German trilled [R]. A
GLOTTAL is formed by briefly closing the glottis: "uh-oh!" and
is symbolized by a question mark without the lower dot, [ʔ]. A
PHARYNGEAL is formed by partially closing the pharyngeal walls
and aspirating strongly, as in clearing the throat, like [H].

As in the case of the vowel positions, the consonant positions
are approximate rather than exact. For example, the French
[t] is generally a dental stop, with the tip of the tongue against
the teeth, while the American [t] is generally an alveolar stop.
American [d] is an alveolar stop, but in Spanish [d] is more of a
dental stop. American [r], a relatively weakly stressed consonant,
can be made in a number of positions. It may even occur in a
retroflex position, with the tip of the tongue curled slightly
backward. In British English, the [r] often has a flapped quality
that resembles [d]; so British "very" sounds like "veddy."

Continuants are further classified as FRICATIVES, NASALS,
LIQUIDS, LATERALS, and GLIDES. As the name indicates, fricative
means friction, and derives from the formation of these phones
through a constriction somewhere along the vocal tract. Fricatives are also called SPIRANTS. In English, [f] is a labiodental
fricative; [θ] is a dental fricative; [s] is an alveolar fricative;
[ʃ] is a palatal fricative. While English does not have a velar
fricative, other languages do. The consonant *ch* in German
lachen and Yiddish *chutzpah* is formed with the back of the tongue
against the soft palate, or velum, and is symbolized by [x].
Arabic has a pharyngeal fricative produced by tensing the
pharyngeal wall so that the breath comes out with a slightly
rasping sound. Pharyngeal "h" is symbolized in the consonant
tables as [H] to distinguish it from the weaker glottal [h].

Nasals are continuants that pass through the nasal cavity.

In English, [m] is a bilabial nasal, [n] an alveolar nasal, and [ŋ], as in "sing," is a velar nasal. Spanish ñ, as in *señorita*, is alveolar-palatal, while French *gn*, as in *soigner*, is more palatal. Both those sounds are included here under the symbol [ɲ]. Generally speaking, liquids are the sounds, including [l] and [r], which are made laterally from the tongue and are without friction, hence liquid. Other laterals and glides include [w], a bilabial glide, and [ʎ], this last sound a palatal lateral, occurring as *ll* in Spanish *calle* and as *gl* in Italian *figlio*.

Table 5-3 gives the approximate pronunciation of the consonants in Table 5-2.

TABLE 5-3

The Pronunciation of Consonants

[p]	pet (American)	[ç]	ich (German)
[b]	bet (Am)	[ʃ]	ship (Am)
[t]	tore (Am)	[ʒ]	pleasure (Am)
[d]	door (Am)	[x]	hijo (Sp)
[tʃ]	cheer (Am)	[ɤ]	Wagen (Ger)
[dʒ]	jeer (Am)	[h]	him (Am)
[k]	cap (Am)	[H]	Hamid (Ar)
[g]	gap (Am)	[m]	might (Am)
[q]	suq (Arabic)	[n]	night (Am)
[ʔ]	doʔle (Towa)	[ɲ]	soigner (French)
[ß]	caballo (Spanish)	[ŋ]	sing (Am)
[f]	fine (Am)	[R]	carro (Sp)
[v]	vine (Am)	[r]	red (Am)
[θ]	thin (Am)	[ɫ]	łid (Navajo)
[ð]	then (Am)	[l]	lid (Am)
[s]	sip (Am)	[w]	water (Am)
[z]	zip (Am)	[ʎ]	calle (Sp)
		[j]	you (Am)

Two other characteristics serve to divide consonants: VOICED and VOICELESS. Normal breathing occurs when the glottis is open; this is voiceless. When a person gives a prolonged groan, he has closed his glottis and exerted tension on the vocal cords (whether he knows it or not); this is voiced. The phone [s] is voiceless, while its physiological counterpart, [z], is voiced. Many consonants come in pairs, formed in the same position, but one being voiceless and the other voiced. [t] and [d] are pairs, as are [p] and [b], [k] and [g], [f] and [v], [ʃ] and [ʒ], [ɫ] and [l]. A simple way to distinguish between voiced and voiceless phones is to put your hands tightly over your ears and pronounce the contrastive pairs in words. For example, in so pronouncing the words "bet" and "pet," you can hear the "b" clearly, the "p" barely. Two non-English phones are the velar spirants [x] and [ɣ]. The first is voiceless, as in German *ach* [ɑx] and in Spanish *hijo* [ixo]. The second, [ɣ], is voiced, as in German *Wagen* [vɑɣən], Spanish *hago* [aɣo], Arabic *gharb* [ɣɑrb], and Greek *gamma* [ɣama]. As a matter of fact, [ɣ] was present in Old English, being sounded in such words as *saga*, but it no longer appears in Modern English.

Some linguists use alternate symbols for some of these sounds, such as [č] for [tʃ], [š] for [ʃ], [ž] for [ʒ].

Sounds and Meaning

So far, this has been a treatment of phonetics, or the formation of phones—the formation, that is, of speech-sounds as they are actually made. Now to phonemics. The phoneme, we have said, is the speech-sound as it is interpreted. It is the smallest unit of meaningful sound in a given language. For instance, the glottal stop is a meaningful sound in Arabic and a number of Indian languages, but it has no significance nor meaning in American speech. It is the throat-tightening break separating the two sounds in the exclamation "uh-oh!" In Towa, a Pueblo Indian language, /doʔle/, uttered with the glottal stop, means "just fallen down"; /dole/, uttered without the glottal stop, means "might fall." (Note that slashes are used to enclose phonemic transcriptions.) While the glottal stop does occur in certain pronunciations in the United States, it has no real significance from a *meaning* standpoint. In New York City, you may hear "bottle" pronounced as [bɑʔl], but it means exactly the same thing as [bɑdəl], as the word is pronounced in other parts of the country.

Phonemes are further isolated within a given language through CONTRAST. In English, the phones "p" and "b" are in contrast; therefore, they are different phonemes. The word "pit" is separate in meaning from "bit"; "pet" is separate in meaning from "bet." This contrast does not occur in all languages, though. An Arab student at an American university, for example, might say, "I'd like some beach bie," and his American friends would know he meant, "I'd like some peach pie." The sounds do not contrast in his language; therefore, they are not phonemic. Unless he is drilled in the sound-difference, he will not even hear the difference, because it bears no meaning for him. In some Spanish dialects, the "z"-"s" contrast does not occur, as it does in English, so that a Spaniard might say "seal" for "zeal," or "bus" for "buzz." Again, he probably doesn't even hear the difference.

This cultural deafness to nonnative phonemes is one of the first problems to be resolved by the language learner or linguistics student. As a matter of fact, the same inattention to the characteristics of their own native speech-sounds is true of most people. As a simple test, just listen carefully to the people around you, in your own speech community. Do they sound the "r" in words like "car," "care," "park"? Do they pronounce "father" as [fæðɚ] or [faðɚ] or [fɑðɚ]? (The combination of [ə] and [r] is often represented as [ɚ]). For "bought" do they say [bat] or [bɔt]?

The vast majority of people have never heard their own voices on tape, records, or whatever. The probability is high that few people would recognize their voices the first time they heard themselves on tape. The voice goes out from the speaker, not back to his own ears; consequently, he does not hear himself as others hear him or as he would hear his voice played back on tape. Many speakers do not really hear their annoying "uh, uh, uh" unless it comes back to them from a recording. They do not know that their speech has a strong nasality, or a strong emphasis of glides, or a particularly sibilant pronunciation of "s." What they do hear is their words. The same is generally true of listeners. In conversation, native speakers tune in to the meaning of the message, not to the articulatory characteristics.

Unless it is demonstrated to them, very few Americans are aware of the fact that they pronounce their "p" in different ways, depending upon the speech environment, or the neighboring sounds (see p. 73). The demonstration is simple: Hold your open palm a couple of inches from your mouth, then pronounce the words "pit" and "spit." A puff of air accompanies the "p" of "pit," but does not accompany the "p" of "spit." Due to its initial position, the first "p" is ASPIRATED. The second is unaspirated. With a bit of practice, you can pronounce the initial "p" just as you do the medial one (and then yours will sound like the unaspirated French pronunciation of *p*). The significance, from a phonemic standpoint, is that in English the two sounds are the same in meaning, as is also the unreleased "p" in "riptide." The following list illustrates the phonetic differences as constrasted with the phonemic similarities:

	Phonetic	Phonemic
Strong aspiration	[pʰɪt]	/pɪt/
Medium aspiration	[p'ɪt]	/pɪt/
Unaspirated	[sp⁼ɪt]	/spɪt/
Unreleased	[rɪp⁻taɪd]	/rɪptaɪd/

Such variants of a phone are called ALLOPHONES. A phoneme, then, is not a single sound, but a small family of sounds with slight, nonmeaningful differences. In the chapter on dialect, we discussed regional and other causes contributing to differences in pronunciation among speakers of the same language. We also discussed *idiolects*, the differences in speech among even closely related individuals. The word "silk" is pronounced a variety of ways, depending upon the linguistic backgrounds of the speakers, their individual characteristics, and other factors. It is generally, but not always, transcribed phonemically as /sɪlk/. However, this is a phonemic convenience, rather than a phonetic accuracy. All native Americans would interpret the word the same upon hearing it, even with its allophonic variations. The phone [ɪ], as we saw in Table 5-2, is formed in the high front part of the mouth. Actually, more people pronounce the "i"

FIGURE 5-3

Three Allophones of "I"

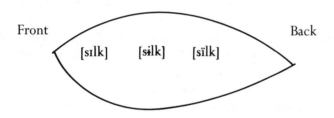

in "silk" as [ɨ], a phone which is formed high in the mouth, but farther back toward the center than [ɪ]. Still others pronounce it as [ï], a phone formed high like the other two allophones, but still farther back in the mouth than [ɨ]. Figure 5-3 illustrates the relative positions of these three allophones.

For another example of allophones, take the word "bird" and see how many different pronunciations you can give to the vowel sound and still have the word recognized by a friend as "bird." We transcribe the word phonemically as /bərd/ or /bɚd/. A phonetician, taking note of the allophonic variations, however, would give the transcription a far more refined notation, using symbols which we have not included on our diagrams.

Again, the easiest way to recognize *allophones*—as well as other speech phenomena discussed in this book—is to listen carefully to people talking, and particularly to the differences in the way they talk.

Certain allophones are in COMPLEMENTARY DISTRIBUTION. That is, they are limited to the environment in which they occur, and do not appear in other environments. For example, the [ḵ] of "keep"—/kip/—is a front palatal stop, raised and fronted under the influence of the following high vowel, [i]. In contrast is the velar stop, [ḵ], of "calm"—/kɑlm/. The latter allophone is under the influence of the low back vowel [ɑ]. Palatal [ḵ] does not occur in "calm," nor does velar [ḵ] occur in "keep." Thus, they are in complementary distribution in English. Likewise, the phoneme /ə/ occurs as two allophones in complementary distribution; one is stressed, as in [kʌp], "cup," and the other is unstressed, as in [ǽpɔ̌l], "apple." You will be able to get an idea of how complementary distribution works if you try to pronounce "keep" with a low back "k," and "calm" with a high front "k."

It should begin to be pretty clear by now that sounds which are phonemes in some languages are completely absent from other languages. Further, what are allophones in some languages may be distinct phonemes in others. The native American does not hear—or if he does hear, does not attach meaning to—the aspiration or nonaspiration of "p." A Chinese listener, however, would hear two distinctly different sounds, two separate phonemes. In Chinese, *pù* (unaspirated) means "cloth," while *p'ù* (aspirated) means "a bed." *Tō* (unaspirated) means "many," but *t'ō* (aspirated) means "to take off."

The best way to test for phonemic contrast is to set up MINIMAL PAIRS, or structures in which only one phone seems to differ. A minimal pair in English would be "bit" and "pit," two words that have different meanings and yet are similar in shape except for the initial phonemes. We have just seen that Chinese aspirated [p'] contrasts with unaspirated [p⁼], and aspirated [tʼ] with unaspirated [t⁼]. We have also seen that palatal [k̯] and velar [k̩] do not contrast in English. However, they do contrast in Arabic. Palatal *katir* means "abundant," while velar *qatir* means "stingy." Arabic also has contrastive *h*, one a mildly aspirated glottal fricative like the American [h] in "hello," the other a strongly aspirated pharyngeal fricative, symbolized by [H]. Thus, glottal *habba* means "to love," and pharyngeal *habba* means "to storm." (Possibly this is the source of English "hubbub.") The Spanish trilled *r*, symbolized by [R], has phonemic value in that language. A commonly cited minimal pair is *pero* ("but") and *perro* ("dog"). Another is *caro* ("expensive") and *carro* ("cart").

Nasality does not have phonemic value in English. If an American says [hæt], we recognize that he is saying "hat," but only notice casually that he is "talking through his nose." However, nasalization has phonemic value in some American Indian languages, including Towa. In this language, *kwį* (nasalized) means "wind," and *kwi* (nonnasalized) means "a light."

In Chinese, as well as in some other languages, mainly Oriental, tone has phonemic value. Tonality is what gives Chinese its so-called sing-song quality. By changing the tone at each production, the same word may have several entirely different meanings. The word *pān*, spoken with a high-level tone, means "class"; *păn*, with a dipping tone, means "board"; *pàn*, with a falling tone, means "half."

In normal speech, phonemes seldom occur in isolation, but always in motion and in association with other phonemes. The vocal organs are constantly moving, not stopping to break out phoneme by phoneme. The phonemes seem to flow together, particularly to the ear of the nonnative. That is one reason why beginners in a new language complain that the native speakers "talk too fast." These vowel and consonant phonemes occur in a chainlike sequence of linked segments, and so they are called SEGMENTAL PHONEMES. Besides the segmental phonemes, however, speech consists of other characteristics which signal meaning to the listener. These characteristics are called SUPRA-SEGMENTAL PHONEMES. They consist of JUNCTURE, PITCH, and

STRESS; together they all make up the INTONATION PATTERN of speech.

Juncture is the slight pause between elements—syllables, words, sentences—which is usually more anticipated than actually heard by the native speaker. A native American intuits, or senses, the difference between two such utterances as:

I must see Mable tonight.
I must seem able tonight.

Of course, his intuition is aided by the context of such utterances. He also senses the difference between:

It's a nice house.
It's an ice house.

But even to the native speaker confusion may sometimes arise over just where in spoken language the juncture belongs. In Old English, the word for "snake" was pronounced and spelled *nœdre*. Up through Middle English it was *nadder*. But sometime after about 1500, *a nadder* became *an adder*. The same confusion over juncture accounts for today's spelling of "a nickname." In Old English it was *an eacanama* ("an additional name"). But in Middle English it was spelled *a nekename*.

A word, then, is actually a semantic unit concerned with meaning far more than it is a phonetic unit concerned with pronunciation. When words are written out, it is easy enough for us to see the juncture—simple separation of words by spaces. But in speech, it is not so easy to make these separations. We listen for meaning, not for mechanics. This particular area of phonetics, juncture, is called COMBINATORY PHONETICS. It concerns itself with such phenomena as assimilation. Assimilation occurs through environmental influence (see p. 73). An example in English would be the rapidly spoken utterance: "Did you see it?" The final "d" of "did" assimilates to the "y" of "you," resulting in the phoneme /dʒ/, thus /dɪdʒu si ɪt/.

Another example: Most Americans, when they ask, "What's your name?" quite rapidly, come out with something like "Whachername?"—/hwatʃənem/. This type of assimilation is called SANDHI, a Sanskrit word which means "binding together." In French, the article *le* and the nominal *homme* combine with a double loss: the *h*, which is regularly silent, and the terminal *e* of *le*—producing *l'homme*—/lom/, "the man."

Some years ago I was thoroughly confused by just such an example of sandhi, in conversation with a slangy young French friend. My friend interrupted the conversation suddenly to point across the street and exclaim: "*Regardez steep là!*" It took a few moments of question and answer before it became clear to me that he was saying, not "steep," but "*ce type*," equivalent to "that character."

The phonemic nature of juncture is clearly illustrated by such examples as "a nice house"–"an ice house." In this case the juncture controls the meaning; therefore, the juncture itself is phonemic.

Pitch is caused by the varying rapidity of vibration of the vocal cords. The more rapid the vibration, the higher the pitch. Changing the pitch frequency results in a change of tone. We have seen that pitch, or tone, is phonemic in Chinese and other tonal languages. It can also be phonemic in English. Phoneticians generally consider that English speakers use four tones, roughly analogous to the music class' "do-mi-sol-do." Unlike musical tones, which are exactly pitched, the tones of speech are relative. In transcription, syllables may be numbered 1, 2, 3, 4, with 1 generally indicating the lowest pitch and 4 the highest. Or a line may be drawn through the utterance, showing the pitch contour:

² ² ³¹ ²¹
Pete went fishing today.

Pete went fishing today.

Unlike Chinese, pitch in an isolated English word plays no part in meaning. The word "out" has the same meaning, whether pronounced in a high tone, a low tone, a rising tone, or a falling tone. The difference in meaning occurs grammatically in a full utterance and in a particular context, as when the coach shouts, "He's out?" and the umpire shouts back emphatically, "He's out!"

The third suprasegmental phoneme, stress, is the loudness or softness of speech utterances. The four stress phonemes of English are symbolized by /´/ for loudest, /^/ for next loudest, /ˋ/ for normal stress, and /ˇ/ for weak. Phonemic stress can be illustrated by the difference in pronunciation and meaning of "subject" the noun, and "subject" the verb: "súbjĕct"-"sŭbjéct." There are many other noun-verb contrasts in English: "réfŭse"-"rĕfúse," "súrvĕy"-"sŭrvéy," "pérmĭt"-"pĕrmít," and so on. In Spanish, stress can have an even more complex grammatical function. *Cánto* means "I sing," but *cantó* means "he sang." *Cánto* also means "song." *Río* means "I laugh," *rió* means "he laughed," and *río* means "river." In Spanish, these marks are included in the spelling.

Phonemic stress is not a characteristic of all languages. Languages with FIXED STRESS may use stress when emphasizing a point or when displaying anger or some other emotion, but the stress is not phonemic—it does not determine the meaning of a word, as the stress in "súbjĕct"-"sŭbjéct" does. Among languages with fixed stress are French, which always places the stress on the last syllable; Finnish and Hungarian, which always stress the first syllable; and Polish, which always stresses the *penultimate*, or next to last syllable. Languages in which the stress does shift from syllable to syllable with different phonemic values are called FREE STRESS languages. They include English, Spanish, Russian, and Greek, among others.

We have noted repeatedly that what is a phonemic distinction in one language is not necessarily a phonemic distinction in another. A field linguist just beginning to transcribe a completely unknown language must at first treat every separately articulated phone as if it were a phoneme. Aspirated and unaspirated phones are carefully noted, using the appropriate phonetic symbols. Glottal stops are recorded. Dental "t" is transcribed separately from palato-alveolar "t," long vowels are noted separately from short vowels. Obviously, the linguist is getting down a great deal more than he will ultimately need, but in the beginning he can take no chances. (Such attention to fine distinctions can get ridiculous. I once began working on a project including transcribing a hitherto unwritten language, only to discover after about a month that my chief informant had a lisp.)

After the linguist has gathered a great deal of data, including all the phones as they occur in different environments, he begins to contrast the slightly different phones to determine whether they are allophones of the same phonemes, or totally different phonemes. Does, for example, prepalatal [y] contrast with postpalatal [u]? In English, they are regional allophones; some dialects say [nyzpepɚ] and others, [nuzpepɚ]. If they turn out to be allophones in the target language, then the linguist may scratch the collection of phonetic symbols he has gathered for that sound and put just one phonemic symbol in his developing phonemic alphabet. But if they contrast, as in French /dəsu/ ("below"), /dəsy/ ("above"), then they must be noted as two phonemes. If he finds two similar but not identical phones in complementary distribution (see p. 102), such as [ʌ] in stressed positions and [ə] in unstressed positions, he classifies them as a single phoneme, /ə/. There are, of course, other refinements in the analysis of field notes, but this much will serve as an introduction.

It is easy to see how and why strong "foreign accents" show up in the speech patterns of learners of other languages. The Frenchman, with his fixed stress on the final syllable, refers to the "gangstérs of Chicagó." The American carries over into French the low back /ɑ/ and diphthong /eɪ/ to produce /dʒə pɑrl frɑnseɪ/. The Spaniard, lacking the phoneme /ʃ/, announces he will wear a sport /tʃɚt/ to the outing. And in Hawaii and parts of the Mainland, the Oriental's mixing of /l/ and /r/ has resulted in the good-humored expression "Rots of ruck."

FOR FURTHER READING

Gudschinsky, Sarah C., *How to Learn an Unwritten Language*. New York: Holt, Rinehart and Winston, 1967.

Malmberg, Bertil, *Phonetics*. New York: Dover, 1963.

Pike, Kenneth L., *Phonemics: A Technique for Reducing Language to Writing*. Ann Arbor: University of Michigan Press, 1964.

Samarin, William J., *Field Linguistics: A Guide to Linguistic Field Work*. New York: Holt, Rinehart and Winston, 1967.

Thomas, Charles K., *An Introduction to the Phonetics of American English*, 2nd ed. New York: Ronald Press, 1958.

The area of morphology is one in which languages tend to display a considerable amount of irregularity, especially if one does not pry beneath the surface.

Ronald Langacker

6

MORPHOLOGY

A Closer Look at Words

Just as phonemes are the smallest units of meaningful sound, MORPHEMES are the smallest units of meaningful form (Greek *morphe* = "form"). These units may consist of words; they may also consist of parts of words. And here it should be admitted that while we use the term *word* freely, at present we really have no absolute concept or definition of *word*. The morpheme, then, is the smallest grammatical unit, and MORPHOLOGY is the study of morphemes.

The unit may stand alone, in which case it is a FREE MORPHEME, or it may have to be attached to another unit, in which case it is a BOUND MORPHEME. The word "gentle" may stand alone; so can the word "man." They combine to form the word "gentleman." To this combination we add "-ly," creating the adjective "gentlemanly." The whole concept may be changed by adding "un-" to the word: "ungentlemanly." "-Ly" and "un-" are bound morphemes; they cannot stand alone, yet they carry full grammatical meaning.

The morpheme which carries the basic meaning of a word is called the BASE or ROOT, while the bound morpheme attached to it is called the AFFIX. "Swift" in "swiftly" is the base, and "-ly" is the affix. In this case the affix is a SUFFIX, because it is attached to the *end* of the base. "Un-" in "ungentle" is a PREFIX, being attached to the *front* of the base.

Some of our words break apart into their morphemic constituents more readily than others, and are thus more recognizable as separable units. For example, "unwisely" is easily separated into its base, "wise," and its adverbial suffix, "-ly," and its negative prefix, "un-." "Wise" is used frequently in general discourse. Less easily recognized would be "ungainly," if it were broken down into its base and affixes, or even if the negative prefix were removed. Although "gain" in the sense of profit or achievement is commonly known, less common is "gainly" in the sense of suitable or graceful; and we just don't break "gainly" down to "gain" and "-ly."

Many other affixes were formerly separate in Old English and its Germanic ancestor. *Had* was a free morpheme, meaning condition or state of being. It very early became a bound morpheme; later it began to be pronounced and spelled as "hood." We still have such words as "childhood" and "brotherhood," the suffix deriving from the old free morpheme *had*. The same is true of *lic*, earlier a separate adjective meaning what it appears to be: "like" or "similar." Modern "slowly" was formerly *slaw-lice*, the *lice* eroding in pronunciation and spelling and gradually becoming a bound morpheme. However, we still use both forms of the suffix, as in the adjectives "manly" and "manlike." Some prefixes have developed through this same process. When Thomas Malory wrote his story of King Arthur in late Middle English, he used the two separate words *on live* to express the condition of living. In the past five hundred years, *on live* went to *on-live* to *a-live* to "alive."

Morphemes are sometimes spoken of as FULL and EMPTY. Full morphemes mainly include nouns, verbs, adjectives, and adverbs—items that are classed as CONTENT WORDS, or CONTENTIVES. These items have semantic content, or individual meaning. STRUCTURE WORDS, or FUNCTORS, consisting of articles, prepositions, conjunctions, are empty morphemes. They are structurally necessary to form sentences, but are empty of semantic content. In one sense, we can consider them as bound forms, although they appear to stand alone. The article "the" cannot appear in a phrase structure without a following noun; the noun, however, can appear alone. We can say, "The cats are noisy tonight," and "Cats are often noisy at night," but we cannot say, "The are noisy tonight."

Affixes are generally grouped with empty morphemes. However, the distinction between full and empty is not always a clear one, and such a classification should be handled with caution. We appear to have two distinct full morphemes in "dogwood"; yet when "dog" is separated from "wood," the latter will stand with its full meaning of "wood," but "dog" has lost all its apparent meaning in this environment. On the other hand, a very definite bound morpheme such as the agentive "-er" cannot truly be said to be empty of semantic force. There is an obvious semantic distinction between "swim" and "swimmer"—one is an act, the other is an actor.

Another pitfall to be looked out for is the similar shape of two totally different forms. While "-er" in "swimmer," "trader," "actor" ("-er" and "-or" are the same form, though spelled differently) is a clear-cut morpheme, although a bound one, "-er" in "anger," "mother," "butter," and the like is not a morpheme. The native speaker of English senses this distinction, but a nonnative speaker—or learner—could be confused by such apparent similarities.

A more definite typing of morphemes is the separation of affixes into DERIVATIONAL and INFLECTIONAL. While derivational affixes modify the word lexically, or according to its dictionary meaning, inflectional affixes modify the word grammatically. The following paradigm illustrates the derivational process:

child	(noun)
childhood	(noun)
childlike	(adjective)
childish	(adjective)
childishness	(noun)
childishly	(adverb)
unchildishly	(adverb)

The base, "child," moves into the different form classes of adjective, noun, and adverb by the affixing of bound morphemes. By the same rule, the base morpheme "swim," a verb, is moved into another form class, becoming a noun by the affixing of "-er." "Real," an adjective, is transformed into a noun by the affixing of "-ity."

Inflectional affixes, on the other hand, do not shift a base into another form class, but modify it for grammatical signals such as number, person, gender, and so on. The following Latin paradigm shows number, person, tense, and voice in the inflectional suffixes:

porto	I carry	*portamus*	we carry
portas	you carry	*portatis*	you carry
portat	he, she, it carries	*portant*	they carry
portabo	I will carry	*portabimus*	we will carry
portabis	you will carry	*portabitis*	you will carry
portabit	he, she, it will carry	*portabunt*	they will carry

We see plainly enough from this paradigm that Latin is a heavily inflected language, while English is much less so. Instead of having affixes to indicate the grammatical relationships shown in the paradigm, English depends mostly on separate auxiliary elements, including separate personal pronouns. While the

Latin item has an inflectional change in every instance, the English has only one: third-person singular, present tense adds a terminal "-s."

A further example showing the loss of inflection in Modern English (Old English was highly inflected) is the following comparison with some other Indo-European languages which have retained much of their inflectional systems:

English	Spanish
the old man	*el viejo hombre*
the old men	*los viejos hombres*
the good girl	*la buena señorita*
the good girls	*las buenas señoritas*

French	German
le viel homme	*der alte Mann*
les vieux hommes	*die alter Männer*
la bonne fille	*das gut Mädchen*
les bonnes filles	*die güte Mädchen*

In English, the article and the adjective retain the same form whether the nominal (or noun) is masculine or feminine, singular or plural. In the other languages, inflectional changes occur within the article and adjective, as well as within the nominal, to assure CONCORD, or agreement among the article, the adjective, and the nominal. Inflectional changes do occur in English in the nouns themselves, generally the affixing of the plural morpheme "-s." But this morpheme may vary, as we will see later.

Just as the families of phonemes have their phonetic variations, called allophones, so morphemes have variations, which are called ALLOMORPHS. These allomorphs consist mainly of phonetic variations within a morpheme class. The variations are usually caused by the phonetic environment of the particular morpheme, as we shall see, and they may or may not be indicated by a different spelling. Those variations resulting from environmental influence are known as MORPHOPHONEMIC ALTERNATIONS.

The plural morpheme in English, generally symbolized by {S-1} or {Z-1},[1] has five allomorphs. Pronounce the three plural words "cats," "dogs," "horses," and you will produce the three most common plural allomorphs. But notice carefully that although the spelling of the inflectional endings of the three words is essentially the same, the pronunciation is totally different. The first, "cats," ends in /s/; the second, "dogs," ends in /z/; and the third, "horses," ends in /ɨz/. If we were writing a set of rules for our morphophonemic alternations, we would have to indicate that /s/ occurs after a voiceless stop, as in "cats," "minks,"; /z/ occurs after a voiced stop or continuant, as in "dogs," "tigers," "lions"; /ɨz/ occurs after voiced and voiceless sibilants, as in "horses," "roses," "bushes."

A fourth plural allomorph comprises a group of irregular, unpredictable forms, including such plurals as "ox"-"oxen," "man"-"men," "goose"-"geese," "child"-"children." While the three allomorphs /s/, /z/, and /ɨz/ are conditioned by their linguistic environment, this group is not so conditioned. We might symbolize them collectively as /ən/. The fifth plural allomorph is the zero, symbolized by /ø/, representing the absence of change in such plural forms as "sheep"-"sheep," "fish"-"fish," "deer"-"deer."

As well as the {S-1} class for plural allomorphs, there are two other morpheme classes which are identical to it in phonetic shape—/s/, /z/, /ɨz/—but different in meaning. They are the possessive morpheme, {S-2}, as in "the ship's course," "the man's hat," "the horse's mouth"; and the third-person-singular morpheme, {S-3}, as in "she walks," "he carries," "the elephant dances."

The same sort of phonetic variations appear as allomorphs in the past-tense morpheme, {D-1}. The endings for "fished," "grazed," "granted" are spelled the same, but are phonetically different, occurring as /fɪʃt/, /grezd/, /græntɨd/. These suffix

---

[1] The brace, { }, is used to enclose a morphemic symbol.

morphemes indicate the past tense of English regular verbs. Irregular verbs are like the irregular nouns in the unpredictability of their morphemes. In these verbs, past tense is signaled by vowel changes, or even complete word replacement, as "go"-"went," "ride"-"rode," "give"-"gave," "am"-"was," "creep"-"crept," "sing"-"sang" (see *ablaut*, pp. 65–66). A symbolic paradigm for the past-tense morpheme class would be indicated in part as follows:

$$\{\text{D-1}\} = /t/ \sim /d/ \sim /\text{id}/ \sim /i \rightarrow \varepsilon/ \sim /i \rightarrow \text{æ}/^2$$

A simple framework such as the following illustrates a small part of the English inflectional system, as well as the relationship between content words and function, or structure, words:

The _____s _____ed in the _____s.

The bound morphemes act as structure signals; the first "-s," by its position following the article "the," signals a plural noun; the "-ed" signals a past-tense verb; and the final "-s," by its position following the preposition and article "in the," signals another plural noun. The skeleton structure may be filled in with an almost infinite number of content morpheme forms, such as:

The cows grazed in the meadows.
The boys fished in the streams.
The frogs feasted in the bogs.
The Martians landed in the fields.

In some languages concord is reflected morphologically not only in articles, adjectives, and nominals, but also in verbs. Such verb inflection is shown in the following examples:

---

2 The marker $\sim$ indicates alternation.

English

The hunter hurried across the field.
The three hunters hurried across the fields.

German

Der Jäger eilte über das Feld.
Die drei Jäger eilten über die Felder.

Spanish

El cazador se apresuró a través del campo.
Los tres cazadores se apresuraron a través de los campos.

French

Le chasseur se dépêcha à travers du champ.
Les trois chasseurs se dépêchèrent à travers des champs.

The same morphemic sets do not necessarily occur in different languages. Some speech communities do not feel the need for certain grammatical elements. As indicated in the examples shown, English does not have a need to express concord by making articles and adjectives plural, nor by making verbs plural. (A distinction is made between singular and plural in the third person, present tense.) On the other hand, certain languages reflect a need for grammatical elements which other speech communities may never even think of. Arabic, for example, has suffixes which indicate not only whether the party addressed is singular or plural, but also whether the party is a male or a female. In Arabic, "You sit down, please" is expressed as follows:

	Singular		Plural
(masc.)	ijlis, min faɒlak	(m. and f.)	ijlisuw, min
(fem.)	ijlisiy, min faɒlik		faɒlikum

Likewise, the query "What is the name of your son?" is modified according to whether the query is addressed to a woman or a man:

(masc.) aysh ism ibnak?   (ibn = "son")
(fem.)   aysh ism ibnik?

Another grammatical element which functions in many languages is the *dual* formation, which vanished from English over a millennium ago. In Arabic, the dual morpheme occurs as a suffix, while the plural morpheme is an INFIX, or an internal phonetic change:

	Singular (one)	Dual (two)	Plural (three or more)
book	kitab	kitabayn	kutub
door	bab	babayn	abwab
woman	hourma	hourmatayn	harim

The dual is also present in many of the American Indian languages, one of them being Towa. The morphemic differences are shown in the following set:

There is a dog.	kæ?nu̜ é	(kæ?nu̜ = "dog")
There are two dogs.	kæ?nu̜ ʃiŋ lé	
There are three dogs.	kæ?nu̜ ʃi é	

As stated earlier, different speech communities have different types of morphemic elements. While the Arabic paradigm just above displays morphemic variation for number only, the Towa morphemes are a bit more complex. In most, if not all, Indian languages the nouns are singular. That is, an Indian would say, "One horse, two horse, three horse," not "One horse, two horses, three horses." In this sense, Indian languages are even less inflected than English. In Towa, then, the basic noun does not change form to indicate number. Number is signaled by other elements in the structure. And other morphemes besides number indicators are also present. The morpheme *é* is a Towa marker indicating an existing situation, a state of being. Thus, a literal translation of the paradigm would be:

kæʔnų		é
dog		exists
kæʔnų	[ʃiŋ	ļé[3]
dog	two	exist
kæʔnų	[ʃi]	é
dog	three or more	exist

Another example of a non-Indo-European need for a particular morphemic element is the classifier, used in many languages, including Vietnamese and Chinese. (To be accurate, a type of classifier does appear in several English structures: a "*fleet* of ships," a "*crowd* of people," a "*flock* of sheep," and so on.) In Vietnamese, anything counted is expressed in a phrase consisting of a number morpheme and a classifier morpheme, plus the nominal itself. For example:

four cats	bôn con mèo = four + living thing + cat
three eating bowls	ba cái bát = three + nonliving thing + eating bowl
two newspapers	hai tờ báo = two + sheet + newspaper

In Chinese, as in Towa, a separate morpheme is used as a question indicator. In the Mandarin greeting *Ní hǎo ma?* the *ma* particle is a question marker. Literally translated into English, the polite greeting would be "You well, eh?" The

---

[3] The brackets are used simply to indicate what part of the structure signals number. In speech, the *ļé* segment is a run-on, just like "they're" in English.

Towa greeting places the question marker first: hæ he é? Literally translated, this would be:

Question marker + "sitting" + state-of-being marker

An approximate equivalent in English would be "You're just sitting?"

Types of Languages

These are just a few examples of the tremendous variety of morphemes in the thousands of languages spoken by the peoples of this earth. Linguists have tried since the early nineteenth century to classify languages into types on the basis of morphological similarities. Languages with isolated morphemes, such as Chinese, are classified as ANALYTIC. Each morpheme has a separate lexical meaning or grammatical force; they are not bound to each other. There are separate morphemes for plural, for possessive, for interrogative, and so on. Thus, "This is my book" in Mandarin is:

Chê   shìh   wǒ   tê   shū
This + is + I + possessive + book
                    particle

and "Are these your books?" is:

Chê   hsiēh   shū   shìh   nǐ   tê   ma
This + plural + book + is + you + possessive + question
       particle   particle   particle

Chinese is probably the closest to a perfect analytic language of all the languages; it rarely has more than one morpheme per word. English is quite analytic, but as indicated by the comparison with equivalent Chinese phrases, it has inflection in the pronouns; Chinese does not.

Highly inflected languages are classified as SYNTHETIC. Such a language is classical Latin (see p. 112). Not nearly as inflected as Latin, but more so than English, are French, Spanish, and German (see pp. 113 and 116).

Two other classes based on morphology are AGGLUTINATIVE and POLYSYNTHETIC. Many non-Indo-European languages fall into the agglutinative class, such as Turkish, Hungarian, Dravidian, Japanese, and, probably, Basque. In these languages, morphemes are joined together in grammatical constructions; but whether bound or free, the morphemes are unchanged when combined with different elements. For example, the plural suffix in an agglutinative language would never vary as much as in English "cat"-"cats," "man"-"men," "horse"-"horses." In an agglutinative language, the plural suffix would remain practically the same in any combination; the base, too, would be unchanged. It must be mentioned, however, that in some of the agglutinative languages—Turkish, for instance—a morphophonemic alternation occurs in the suffixes to produce VOWEL HARMONY, with the suffix echoing the vowel sound of the base. Vowel harmony is observable in the following Turkish nouns:

	Singular	Plural
horse	*at*	*atlar*
city	*šehir*	*šehirler*
house	*ev*	*evler*
room	*oda*	*odalar*
girl	*kiz*	*kizlir*

The agglutinative forms, then, are similar in principle to the inflected forms, but with much less irregularity in the affixes and in the bases. This is true in verb inflection, also. In Turkish, regularity is maintained in the base morpheme *gör*, even when the tense changes:

I see	*görürüm*
I saw	*gördüm*
one who has seen	*görmüs*

By contrast, a complete change is possible even in the same tense in Latin, a synthetic language:

I wish	*volo*
you wish	*vis*
he wishes	*vult*

Or in Spanish, also a synthetic language:

I can	*puedo*	we can	*podemos*
you can	*puedes*	you can	*podéis*
he can	*puede*	they can	*pueden*

Since irregularity occurs in some English verbs, such as "go"-"went"-"gone," English too must be considered somewhat inflectional.

Polysynthetic means "more than usually synthetic." That is, instead of separate words in a sentence being inflected up to a point, as in synthetic languages, in polysynthetic languages one word is inflected by the addition of bound morphemes until it becomes the entire sentence. This classification was added to the traditional three—analytic, synthetic, agglutinative—to describe the Eskimo and American Indian languages. In this structural type, certain concepts which are generally taken for granted in English—subject, object, verb—have no separate existence. Tense may be added as an inflectional morpheme to the noun rather than to the verb.

In Eskimo, we may start with the base word for "a house" and build upon it:

igdlo = a house
igdlorssuaq = a large house
igdluliorpoq = he builds a house
igdlorssualiorpoq = he builds a large house

This word-sentence begins with the stem, which is the fundamental concept, and ends with the personal-pronoun suffix. So the last utterance would translate into something like: "a-house-large-builds-he."

In Navajo, the stem of the verb is the last syllable of the verb. This part of the total structure expresses the verbal idea, often in an abstract manner quite alien to the speaker of Indo-European languages. To this stem are prefixed the morphemic indicators for person, number, adverbial quality. The stem may also change with tense and mode. Thus we get such a construction as:

T ʔáadoó le ʔé	/	shá	/	ádíílííł	/	nisin
thing		for me		you make		I want it

or:

I'd like for you to make something for me.

Such a typological classification as the four discussed, based on morphological criteria, has never proved very satisfactory except in the most general ways. No language fits precisely into one of the four classes. Even Chinese is not completely a one-morpheme–one-word analytic language, nor is Turkish a perfect agglutinative language. And, as at least one disgruntled linguist has pointed out, an Indian construction such as the Navajo one above is often transcribed as a continuum:

T ʔáadoóle ʔésháádíílííłnisin

in order to prove its polysynthetic nature; but in fact it really proves nothing of the sort. One might just as easily transcribe the French construction:

Je ne sais pas où est il

as:

Jen' saispasoùestil

for in fact that is the way it's pronounced.

Does that mean that morphemic theory and practice are invalid? Not at all. Morphemic analysis is one of the most fruitful concepts in the study of language and languages. Every language is a system, and the morphology of a language is part of that system. It simply means that so far no completely satisfactory typological classification of languages has been produced. One proposal for improving upon the morphological classification described in this chapter is a ranking system which would indicate the degree to which a given language is synthetic or analytic. As has been demonstrated, English is partly both.

Another proposal would have languages classified according to their phonological organization. A major division would separate the tonal languages from nontonal languages. The tonal group would include, of course, Chinese, with its pitch phonemes. Further subdivision would be according to other phonological characteristics.

The fact that the present classification system is not 100 percent efficient is no cause for alarm. It has proved very helpful in advancing our knowledge about language. After all, the automobile, which is a central mechanism of our modern culture, runs on a gasoline engine that is only 25 percent efficient.

FOR FURTHER READING

Fries, Charles C., *The Structure of English*. New York: Harcourt Brace Jovanovich, 1952.

Gleason, H. A., Jr., *An Introduction to Descriptive Linguistics*, rev. ed. New York: Holt, Rinehart and Winston, 1961.

Hockett, Charles F., *A Course in Modern Linguistics*. New York: Macmillan, 1958.

Nida, Eugene A., *Morphology: The Descriptive Analysis of Words*, 2nd ed. Ann Arbor: University of Michigan Press, 1949.

All grammars leak.
Edward Sapir

7

GRAMMAR AND SYNTAX

Before defining grammar one must ask, "Which grammar?" To many people, grammar means correctness of language usage. We have all heard from time to time the expressions "He uses good grammar" or "He uses bad grammar." This general concept of grammar refers to all the rules a student must learn regarding such things as subject-verb agreement, whether to use "who" or "whom," and when to use the subjunctive mood. Such a concept puts the term "grammar" in a distasteful light. Upon being introduced in company as an English teacher, I have frequently been greeted with, "Oh, I'd better watch what I say." With a reception like that, an English teacher is not likely to be the life of the party.

Grammar Old and New

Such alarm was more or less warranted in the Middle Ages, for the Old French *gramaire* meant occult learning and magical skill. The word "glamour" is merely a Scottish variant of *gramaire*; and the sense of "bewitching" is still associated with "glamour," as any beauty-aid advertisement makes clear. The magical quality of words is still felt by some cultures; certain names are not pronounced because of ill effects resulting from their use. The name of a dead person is not pronounced by the African Masai or the international Gypsy. Among some American Indians there is a deep feeling that words are very effective in bringing about change and in creating. (Sincere poets in virtually all cultures share this belief.)

Grammar is also used to designate a set of principles governing any body of knowledge, such as the grammar of mathematics or the grammar of music.

From a linguistic point of view, earlier grammarians included just about everything pertaining to language under the heading of grammar: prosody, etymology, orthography, semantics, and so on. At mid-twentieth century, GRAMMAR means the scientific study of the phonological, morphological, and syntactical structure of language.

In analyzing sentences, our grandparents were taught to start out by naming the parts of speech to which the words in the sentence belonged. This was called *parsing*. In recent years, however, the trend in grammatical analysis has shifted from a parts-to-the-whole study of the locution, or sentence, to a viewing of the whole structure first, then a consideration of the parts.

This is the tack taken by the GENERATIVE-TRANSFORMATION-ALIST (G-T) grammarians. They start with the structure of basic sentences and then analyze the sentences down through their structural elements into their smallest phonological elements. Mainly, the G-T's are concerned with underlying principles of language. They interest themselves not just in the surface structure of a locution, or utterance, and how it is organized, but also in the intuitive or native ability a speaker possesses that allows him to utilize the inherent rules of a grammatical system to form acceptable sentences. They wish to write a grammar which will account for this ability.

More interesting work is being done in grammatical analysis and grammatical theory than ever before. The study has been particularly enriched by data from American Indian languages, African languages, and other heretofore unwritten languages. While the work of Noam Chomsky furnishes the basis for G-T studies, a number of different schools have developed in generative grammar. As well as these, the structuralist school, which arose largely from Bloomfield's work, is still flourishing (see Chapter 2). Kenneth L. Pike's school of tagmemics is likewise flourishing; and now a new approach to the study of grammar, called stratificational grammar, has developed. Probably a number of other approaches are on the way. This chapter will present a brief introduction to some of the current approaches. For more detailed study, the student is advised to read any of the recently published introductory books on the subject, a few of which are listed at the end of this chapter.

Interestingly enough, much of the latest in linguistic theory, particularly as it pertains to grammar, goes back to earlier classical concepts of grammar. We have only to go back to 1933 to find one aim of the G-T's already stated in part by Otto Jespersen, one of the truly great scholarly grammarians. A well-constructed grammar, according to Jespersen, "may lead to a scientific understanding of the rules followed instinctively by speakers and writers." Another of the aims of the G-T's, that of discovering a universal deep structure underlying all languages, was expressed by James Harris in 1751 in his *Hermes, or a Philosophical inquiry concerning universal grammar:* a universal grammar would be "that grammar, which without regarding the several idioms of particular languages, only respects those principles, that are essential to them all." Of course, the G-T's are fully cognizant of these earlier inquiries into the nature of grammar.

Much of the still lingering unfavorable affect in regard to grammar, particularly on the part of students, derives from the prescriptivism of grammarians starting from the Renaissance, when English moved into an area of respectability and began to replace Latin as a learned language. These grammarians prescribed what they thought language ought to be, rather than describing what language really was. Latin was still venerated as a "perfect" language, so grammar books, as they began to be written, used Latin as a model for "correct" English usage, ignoring what should have been an obvious fact: that English structure and Latin structure are entirely different. Latin nouns are declined in six cases:

Nominative	*homo*	the man
Genitive	*hominis*	of the man *or* the man's
Dative	*homini*	to the man
Accusative	*hominem*	the man
Ablative	*homine*	from, by the man
Vocative	*homō*	O man!

Latin (as we noted in the preceding chapter) is a highly inflected language; English is not. In each grammatical case in the paradigm above, except the genitive, the English substantive "man" remains the same, uninflected, no matter if it is to be a subject or an object. Yet our early grammarians, still entranced by the influence of Latin declensions, insisted upon giving the English noun six cases likewise. In fact, the English noun has only two case differences in the singular: nominative and genitive, or subjective and possessive—"man," "man's." All other functions are indicated by separate particles, such as articles and prepositions, or by word order.

One advantage—if we wish to regard it as such—of a synthetic language like Latin is its FREE SYNTAX. SYNTAX is that part of a language system having to do with the order of arrangement of words and other morphemes in utterances. In an utterance like "The dog bites the man," it does not matter in a synthetic language what order the elements are arranged in: *Canis mordet hominem*; *Canis hominem mordet*; *Hominem mordet canis*; *Mordet canis hominem*; and so on. In each structure, the function of the two substantives, *canis* and *hominem*, is indicated clearly by their inflectional endings. In an analytic language like English, with its RESTRICTED or BOUND SYNTAX, the function of the substantives must be shown by *word order*. "The man bites the dog" differs considerably in meaning from "The dog bites the man." And in English, one would never hear, "Bites the man the dog." In fact, keeping in mind that syntax is a part of the grammatical structure of a language, we would label this last utterance ungrammatical in English, though not in Latin.

Many linguists have used the familiar structural signals from Lewis Carroll's "Jabberwocky" to illustrate the adequacy of such signals to produce grammatical utterances:

> 'Twas brillig, and the slithy toves
> 　Did gyre and gimble in the wabe:
> All mimsy were the borogoves,
> 　And the mome raths outgrabe.

By establishing a skeletal framework of structural morphemes we get a recognizable set:

> 'Twas _____, and the _____y _____s
> 　Did _____ and _____ in the _____:
> All _____y were the _____s,
> 　And the _____ _____s _____.

To the structuralist school, these structural signals constitute the basis of the grammar of a language. It would seem that, perhaps on a more subconscious level, word order would provide just as much of a set of signals to indicate familiar grammaticality in English. More recent than *Alice in Wonderland* is Anthony Burgess' *A Clockwork Orange*. This first-person narrative is related in a rather odd language created by the author, but after the first few pages the reader is able to get into the swing of the language through a combination of morphological signals and syntactical order. Two examples:

> We itty round, shop-crasting and the like, coming out with a pitiful rookerful of cutter each.

and:

> He was a malenky veck, very fat, with all curly hair curling all over his gulliver, and on his spuddy nose he had very thick otchkies. (From *A Clockwork Orange.* New York: W. W. Norton, 1963. Pp. 52 and 102.)

The first example could be filled in with something like:

> We play around, shop-lifting and the like, coming out with a pitiful handful of loot each.

And the second:

> He was a little man, very fat, with all curly hair curling all over his head, and on his spuddy nose he had very thick glasses.

Less familiar to modern Americans would be the structural and syntactical signals of Old English:

> Ða   genam se   Brihtric him   to   hundeahtatig   scipa.
> Then took   this Brihtric himself for hundred-eighty of ships.

> (Modernized: "Then this Brihtric took for himself a hundred and eighty ships.")

Or Modern German, a cousin of English:

> Ich werde morgen nach Hause gehen.
> I   shall tomorrow to   home   go.

Or Towa:

> John næ æki maʃiˀlɨ mæ.
> John he boy ball gave.

(John gave the ball to the boy.)

Prescriptive and Descriptive Grammar

Just as the phonology, morphology, and syntax differ in different languages, so does the grammar. For the moment we will concern ourselves with some grammatical points in English. First, we need to make some distinctions between PRESCRIPTIVE grammar and DESCRIPTIVE grammar. In general, we think of prescriptive as "bad," as that set of rules imposed upon English grammar by Latin-lovers of the Renaissance and the perfectionists of the eighteenth and nineteenth centuries. We have already discussed the attempt to impose Latin noun cases upon English. We can also cite the imposed rule of "shall" and "will," a rule which we have all had pointed out to us more than once. These two auxiliaries derive from two Old English verbs, *sculan*, meaning "to owe, have to, ought to"; and *willan*, meaning "to wish, choose, intend, desire." By the middle of the seventeenth century, the two verbs had become so mingled in use and meaning that a grammarian, John Wallis, set up arbitrary rules which prescribed their "correct" use. In this case, the rule did not follow usage—and in most cases since it still does not.

But we must not think of prescriptive rules as entirely bad or illogical. In fact, there is considerable overlapping of prescriptive and descriptive grammatical rules. Rules do not have to be written; every language system, by the very fact that it is a system, has rules, whether they are written or not. One such rule is called ANALOGY. Analogy is a process (hence governed by an inherent rule) by which structural patterns are modified or created to conform to existing patterns. It is by this process that most of the strong, or irregular, verbs in Old English have been modified to conform to regular-verb patterns. The young child has his own logic when he exclaims: "Daddy, a bird flied by!" The same logic is causing the gradual change from "old," "elder," "eldest" to "old," "older," "oldest." The process is a constant one; we presently have alternation between "dived" and "dove" for the past tense of "dive." Chances are, "dove" will soon be classified as archaic.

Grammar is constantly changing, and so must the rules which describe it. With the loss of inflection and the increasing importance of word order in English, we are coming around to accepting "who" in the objective case when it occurs in the subjective position. We classify as FORMAL the locution:

Whom did you wish to speak to?

or:

To whom did you wish to speak?

But we are accepting as INFORMAL the structure:

Who did you wish to speak to?

Descriptive grammar, then, is an attempt to describe a language as it actually works. We accept as fact that systematic use of language came long before any specific inquiries into the system itself. People talked before they made rules. In the millennium before Jesus Christ, the ancient Greeks began to notice and label various grammatical elements in their own language; Panini wrote a systematic descriptive grammar of his language, Sanskrit (although it became for succeeding generations a *prescriptive* grammar). In the twentieth century descriptive grammars have been written of hundreds of contemporary languages, including various dialects.

Some Contemporary Grammars

While modern language scientists work toward developing a large body of accurate information about language, they also work toward describing the essentials of language in their simplest forms. For example, structural linguists and G-T linguists agree that all English locutions, no matter how complex, develop from a few basic, or KERNEL, patterns. These patterns are simple, active, declarative statements which, by augmentation and transformation (application of transformation rules), may be made more complex and changed into questions or negations. How many of these basic sentence patterns are there? Linguists list from four to ten or more. Table 7-1 presents some of the groups, with no pretense to completeness.

The kernel sentence patterns in Table 7-1 reveal the BINARY nature of English sentences—and possibly of all languages: each sentence divides into a subject and a predicate. However, we recognize that surface structures, particularly as they are produced in spoken sentences, are often verbless, as in Chinese *Ni hǎo ma?* "You [are] well, eh?"; Russian *Ivan Russky*, "Ivan [is] Russian"; Arabic *Al beyt kibir*, "The house [is] big." Some are subjectless, as in Japanese *Ima dekakemasu*, "[I] now am leaving." In English, we clip sentences down to fragments, such as "Sorry, can't go tonight," in which the "I" is understood.

In syntactical analysis, then, the subject-predicate division has been with us for a very long time. To carry the binary principle further, IMMEDIATE CONSTITUENT (IC) analysis may be applied. This form of analysis, developed by Fries, consists in separating the sentence into two distinct parts, then continuing to separate each part into its two parts until the words or groups of words have been reduced to their constituent morphemes. The structuralists held that this kind of analysis better revealed form classes and constituent relationships than had the traditional system of parsing sentences. Figure 7-1 shows the IC method of analysis.

Reference has already been made to the structural framework of a sentence (see pp. 115 and 129–30). This type of analysis was developed mainly by Charles Fries, who broke from the traditional classification of parts of speech and devised a system of inserting lexical items into the framework on the basis of function. Any item which would function in the position of "men"

TABLE 7-1   Basic Sentence Patterns

	Subject	Verb	Object/Complement	
I	*Subject* Fish	*Intransitive verb* swim.		
II	*Subject* The wolf	*Transitive verb* killed	*Direct object* the deer.	
III	*Subject* The group	*Transitive verb* selected	*Direct object* Bill	*Object complement* their chief.
IV	*Subject* The woman	*Transitive verb* gave	*Indirect object* her friend	*Direct object* a book.
V	*Subject* That horse	*Verb (be)* is	*Subject complement* a winner.	
VI	*Subject* Their father	*Verb (be)* is	*Adjective* tall.	
VII	*Subject* The doctor	*Verb (be)* was	*Adverb* here.	
VIII	*Subject* Eddie	*Linking verb* became	*Subject complement* a student.	
IX	*Subject* Her actions	*Linking verb* seemed	*Adjective* strange.	

FIGURE 7-1

Immediate Constituent Analysis

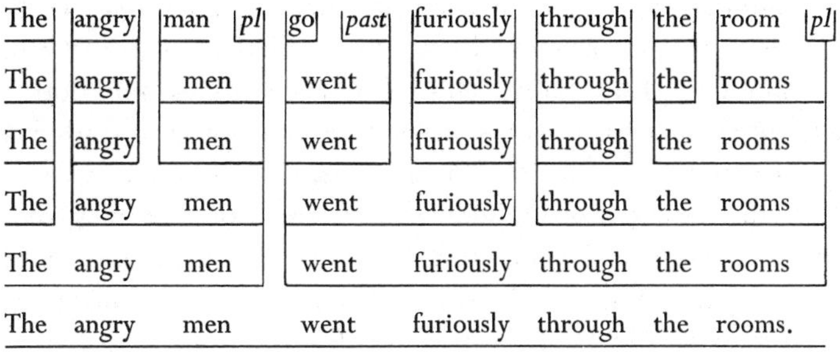

The	angry	man	*pl*	go	*past*	furiously	through	the	room	*pl*
The	angry	men		went		furiously	through	the	rooms	
The	angry	men		went		furiously	through	the	rooms	
The	angry	men		went		furiously	through	the	rooms	
The	angry	men		went		furiously	through	the	rooms	
The	angry	men		went		furiously	through	the	rooms.	

and "room" in the sentence in Figure 7-1 fulfills the function of Form Class I. For example:

The angry *boys* went furiously through the *halls*.

Any item which would function in the position of "went" fulfills the function of Form Class II. For example:

The angry boys *stormed* furiously through the halls.

Any item which would function in the position of "angry" fulfills the function of Form Class III. For example:

The *screaming* boys stormed furiously through the halls.

Finally, any item which would function in the position of "furiously" fulfills the function of Form Class IV. For example:

The screaming boys stormed *angrily* through the halls.

Fries has been criticized, perhaps wrongly, for placing too much emphasis upon structural signals and not enough upon the meaning. What Fries actually stressed, however, was that our foreknowledge of the meaning of a sentence and its constituents too often gets in the way of further analysis of the structural signals. It would be more effective to approach analysis as if the language—be it English or not—were a totally alien one.

Building largely upon Fries' groundwork, Kenneth L. Pike and his associates developed what they called a TAGMEMIC model of grammar. Essentially, this model combines function (or structure) and form (or content) in a basic unit called the *tagmeme* (Greek *tagma* = "arrangement"). For example, the symbolic string S-P-O indicates a functional arrangement: Subject-Predicate-Object. N-V-N indicates a form (or content) arrangement: Noun-Verb-Noun. A tagmemic symbolization of this string would be S:N–P:V–O:N—subject slot filled by a noun phrase, predicate slot filled by a verb phrase, object slot filled by a noun phrase. We might fill these slots with the following or a similar set of items:

S:N	P:V	O:N
The elephants	drank	the water.

The correlation between slot and class designates both form and function; in one position (or slot) the noun phrase is subject; in the other slot, it is object.

An advantage to this system is the classification of elements based upon their meaning as well as their function in a sentence. In the Fries IC model, the two nouns, "elephants" and "water," would simply be designated as Form Class I items.

In the next example, "rowing" at first glance would seem to be simply a verbal, but it obviously functions differently in each of the following structures:

Rowing is good exercise.
The sailor was rowing the boat.
Dad wrecked his rowing machine.

In each structure "rowing" becomes a different tagmeme; meaning is correlated with function.

The tagmemic grammarians go through four steps in constructing their model. Step 1 and Step 2 make up the "discovery" process; Step 3 and Step 4 make up the "verification" process. Step 1 is an empirical step, that of observing the makeup of the language in action. Step 2 is an intuitive step—in effect, guessing at the structure of the data observed. As Charles Hockett says, "Grammatical analysis is still, to a surprising extent, an art: the best and clearest descriptions of languages are achieved not by investigators who follow some rigid set of rules, but by those who through some accident of life-history have developed a flair for it." Step 3 is the formulation of a hypothesis of the language; and Step 4 is a checking of the hypothesis against the facts of the language. Such a model grammar should account for both the grammatical categories (form) and the grammatical relationships (function) of the language.

The tagmemic grammarians also make use of kernel sentences, transformation rules, and the concept of deep structure. They start at the sentence level, and work downward through clause level, then phrase level, then word level. They feel—naturally—that of all the grammatical models in use today, the tagmemic model works best for all languages. Investigators have used it in the analysis of such languages as Vietnamese, various Philippine dialects, and Hindi, as well as English.

Surface Structure and Deep Structure

While we have indicated from time to time the similarities in the views of the various schools of linguists, we must continue to emphasize their main areas of difference. One area in which the G-T's differ with the structuralists is the conceptual, or psychological, aspects of grammar. The G-T's speak in terms of DEEP STRUCTURE as opposed to SURFACE STRUCTURE. They hypothesize that in the realm of deep structure, all languages are fundamentally alike, representing the thought level; languages differ only in their surface structures, which represent actual speech performance. Therefore, the syntactic rules of a complete grammar should accommodate the relationships between conceptual and surface structures. As a simple example, we should consider that the locution "Jerry ate the cherry pie that his wife cooked" is derived from a complex conceptual, or deep, structure which comprises two basic sentences: "Jerry ate the cherry pie" and "Jerry's wife cooked the cherry pie."

The G-T's also differ from the structuralists in emphasis on semantic features, or meaning. Not satisfied with the structuralists' stress on structural signals, the G-T's have pointed out that, although the signals of the lines from the "Jabberwocky" "'Twas brillig, and the slithy toves / Did gyre and gimble in the wabe" did *suggest* a good sentence to Alice, the stanza is not truly a good sentence because of its lack of meaning. Structural signals alone can be deceptive. The structural signals of "The book is interesting" and "The thief is stealing" are the same, but any child knows the difference. Likewise, the native speaker knows the difference between "I walked a mile this evening" and "I walked a dog this evening." Or, "They called him a taxi" and "They called him a fool." The question posed by the G-T's is: *How* does the child native speaker know the difference? A foreigner learning English, by drawing on his pattern practice, might say, "I saw the big rock running down the hill." A native speaker would correct him, but on what basis? It is quite correct to say, "I saw the big rock tumbling down the hill." It is also correct to say, "I saw the stream running down the hill." Then why not let the big rock run down the hill? It is no less human than the stream. These are distinctions that the native speaker makes intuitively. It cannot be that he makes such distinctions purely on familiarity with patterns and grammatical signals. So the G-T's have attempted to construct a grammatical model which will duplicate the kind of judgments that native speakers make about their language. Like the tagmemic model, it is expected to produce or generate all the grammatical sentences in a language and no ungrammatical ones.

AMBIGUITY and PARAPHRASE are accounted for in the G-T's model by surface-structure representation and deep-structure representation, in the form of a tree diagram. Ambiguity occurs in a construction which has two possible meanings, such as, "They called him a doctor," or "They are cleaning women." Figure 7-2 examines the second sentence for its two meanings at the deep-structure level.

FIGURE 7-2

Surface Structure and Ambiguity

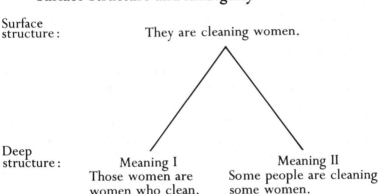

Surface structure: They are cleaning women.

Deep structure:

Meaning I
Those women are
women who clean.

Meaning II
Some people are cleaning
some women.

FIGURE 7-3

Surface Structure and Paraphrase

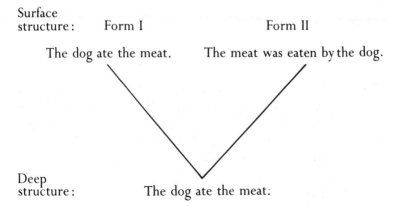

Surface structure: Form I Form II

The dog ate the meat. The meat was eaten by the dog.

Deep structure: The dog ate the meat.

Paraphrase, as Figure 7-3 shows, occurs in a meaning which has two forms, as in the sentences "The dog ate the meat" and "The meat was eaten by the dog."

The deep structures are the basic structures occurring in the mind of the speaker. By a sequence of inherent rules, he *transforms* them into the surface structures—that is, the utterances that he speaks or writes. His innate ability to make such transformations, to construct grammatical utterances, and to distinguish between paraphrases and ambiguous phrases makes up his COMPETENCE. The way he actually speaks is his PERFORMANCE. His competence, or intuitive command of the language, is much greater than his performance.

Starting with the premises that all surface-structure sentences consist of one or more kernel sentences, and that all kernel sentences consist of a noun phrase, an auxiliary, and a verb phrase, the G-T's proceed to analyze these surface-structure sentences back through a series of phrase-structure rules and transformation rules. The first rule,

S → NP + Aux + VP

simply means that "Sentence is rewritten as noun phrase plus auxiliary plus verb phrase." For example, the sentence

The boy eats his lunch.

might be rewritten as,

The boy + tense + eat his lunch.

The auxiliary includes a tense marker (English has only two tenses—present and past) and, optionally, any modal markers required, such as "should," "might," and so on. Unlike German, French, and certain other languages, English has three forms of the present tense—the present simple:

The boy eats his lunch.

the present progressive:

The boy is eating his lunch.

and the present emphatic:

The boy does eat his lunch.

A simple representation of these three forms by tree diagrams is shown in Figure 7-4.

It is readily seen that by a process of substitution, as in the slot-and-filler process (see p. 136), a vast number of sentences may be generated from these three diagrams. Of course, the diagrams have been oversimplified; a more rigorous and detailed analysis would further break down the two NP's into their constituent parts, and a transformation rule would be applied to redistribute the verbal morphemes. Transformation rules have been derived to change statements into questions and negations, and embedding rules and conjoining rules have been derived to construct complex and compound sentences from kernel sentences. Also, morphophonemic rules to account for plural variants; the third-person singular; the possessive case (the allomorphs we discussed in the preceding chapter) have been developed.

A more recent concern is with the semantic aspects of the model grammar. Certain ambiguities still persist which need more rules or more clarification. Also, noun-verb pairing has still not been completely covered. In the LEXICON, or vocabulary inventory of the language, nouns are classified as count, mass, proper, human, nonhuman. Of these, certain classes pair with certain verbs. Thus, referring back to our nonacceptable structure:

I saw the big rock running down the hill.

"rock" would be classified as "count, nonhuman." Acceptable would be:

I saw the stream running down the hill.

FIGURE 7-4

A Tree Diagram

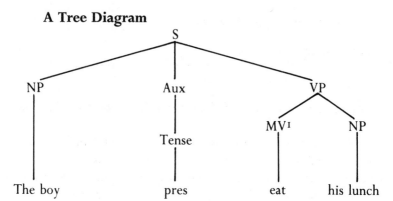

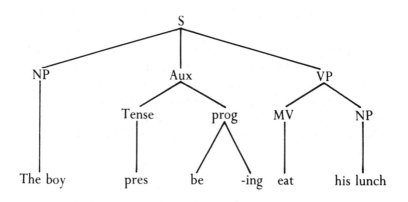

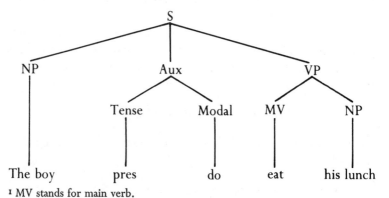

¹ MV stands for main verb.

"Stream" would be classified "mass, nonhuman." Yet "gas" (the vapor) would be classified as "mass, nonhuman," but we could not say:

I saw the gas running down the hill.

In such cases, the G-T's simply write additional rules (if they haven't already) to account for such apparent discrepancies.

Stratificational Grammar

In the mid-1960s, about the time the G-T's had stated that semantics is an integral part of grammar, that even the deep structure of a sentence has to be guided by meaning, a new school of grammarians was developing a different grammar— STRATIFICATIONAL GRAMMAR. Sydney M. Lamb might be called the father of this new approach, which takes full cognizance of thought patterns. He readily admits, however, that much of this "new" approach is based upon observations of earlier linguists. In linguistics as in everything else, the words of the prophet hold true: "There is nothing new under the sun." Language has been with us all the time; we are still trying to discover how it works.

Without attempting a detailed description of the stratificational approach, we can simply say that its exponents view language as a series of layers, or *stratal systems*, all closely related. For example, the phonological strata comprise not only phonemics, but also HYPOPHONEMICS; in the hypophonemic layer lie the physical characteristics of sound—for instance, whether a phone is bilabial, palatal, nasal—and the organic functions which go into the production of phones. By taking into account the speech-making organs as well as the sounds that they produce, we are saying, in effect, that we consider not only the music, but also the musician and his instrument. At the upper strata, which include the meaning, or semantic, layers, are SEMEMICS (sememics is to semantics as phonemics is to phonetics; see pp. 90 and 98), and HYPERSEMEMICS; the hypersememic layers comprise experiential elements—entity, event, process, and other features of meaning. The term "experiential" suggests a memory bank like an electronic computer's. When the human being projects his thoughts as speech, he is making use of the hypersememic

FIGURE 7-5

A Stratum of Relationships[1]

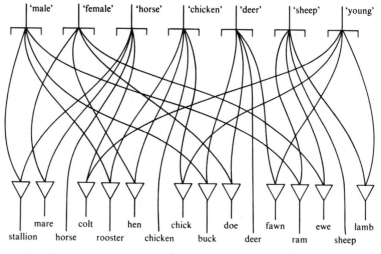

[1] Copyright, © 1972 by Harcourt Brace Jovanovich, Inc., and reprinted with their permission from *Introduction to Stratificational Linguistics*, by David G. Lockwood.

layer—his accumulated experiences, memories, understanding—just as much as of the phonological layer—his speech-making apparatus. Between these two sets of strata lies the grammar set, which includes the morphemic layers; it is here that we retain our awareness of how words are put together.

The stratificational grammarian sees language as a series of contacts across regions, the outermost two being sound and experience. A major difference, then, between stratificational grammar and the others discussed here is its emphasis on experience as a powerful modifying factor in language. Instead of using the tree diagram favored by the G-T's, the stratificationalists use diagrams that resemble the circuitry drawing of an electronic device, or the neural connections of the brain. Figure 7-5 is an example of a stratificational diagram.

We can see, then, that a completely satisfactory grammar has not yet been devised, either for all languages or for one language. As the G-T's state, a satisfactory grammar would provide a model for generating all the grammatical sentences possible in a language, and no ungrammatical ones. Since there is no predictable limit to the number of grammatical sentences in a language, this requirement is a formidable one, perhaps an impossible one. However, our stock of information continues to grow, and linguists are constantly improvising, borrowing, selecting, and rejecting, in their attempt to systematize our knowledge of language.

FOR FURTHER READING

Allen, Robert L., *English Grammars and English Grammar*. New York: Charles Scribner's Sons, 1972.

Cook, Walter A., *Introduction to Tagmemic Analysis*. New York: Holt, Rinehart and Winston, 1969.

Dillard, J. L., *Black English*. New York: Random House, 1972.

Gleason, H. A., Jr., *Linguistics and English Grammar*. New York: Holt, Rinehart and Winston, 1965.

Lester, Mark, *Introductory Transformational Grammar of English*. New York: Holt, Rinehart and Winston, 1971.

Liles, Bruce L., *Linguistics and the English Language*. Pacific Palisades, Calif.: Goodyear Publishing, 1972.

Lockwood, David G., *Introduction to Stratificational Linguistics*. New York: Harcourt Brace Jovanovich, 1972.

What's in a name? That which we call a rose
By any other name would smell as sweet.
                        Romeo and Juliet, II.2.43–44

8

SEMANTICS

Speech is a result of man's ability to see phenomena symbolically. He can make certain things stand for other things, and this we call the symbolic process. But communication demands that two or more people agree on what the symbols stand for. The study of the relationship between symbol and meaning is called SEMANTICS (Greek *semeion* = "mark, sign").

Words and Meanings

Bloomfield describes speech as a sequence of stimuli and responses, the stimuli being the word-symbols of the speaker, and the responses being the interpretation and reaction of the hearer. C. K. Ogden and I. A. Richards have used a triangle to represent the relationship between symbol and referent and meaning, as in Figure 8-1.[1]

If there were a one-to-one relationship between the SYMBOL (word) and the REFERENT (thing), semantics—and communication in general—would be a fairly simple affair. But such is not

FIGURE 8-1

A Semantic Triangle

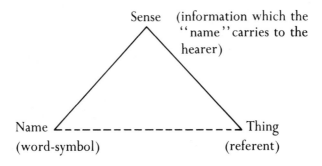

Sense   (information which the "name" carries to the hearer)

Name   (word-symbol)

Thing   (referent)

the case. As well as the linguistic qualities of meaning, there are also philosophical implications, and psychological implications, and logical implications. The very term "meaning" is one of the most ambiguous and controversial terms in the language. Just check the dictionary. You will find such unsatisfying entries as: "that which one wishes to convey," and "that which is felt to be the inner significance of something."

To partly clarify and sharpen the meaning of a word, we use the terms DENOTATIVE and CONNOTATIVE. Denotative refers to the basic or commonly used meaning of a word; connotative refers to the additional, suggested meanings. Consider the different meanings or images suggested by a concrete referent

[1] Adapted from Ogden and Richards, *The Meaning of Meaning*, 8th ed. New York: Harcourt Brace Jovanovich, 1946. P. 11.

like a house, when the symbol "house" is uttered: a home, a fraternity house, the House of Representatives, an astrological term, and so on. Similarly with the symbol "chair." Some would think of a straight-back, wooden chair at a dining table; others

FIGURE 8-2

An Associative Field

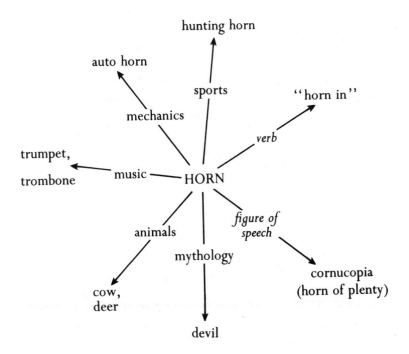

would think of a comfortable stuffed chair; still others might think of the verb "chair," as to chair a committee. The word could also suggest a symbol within a symbol, as when a person at a committee meeting "addresses the chair," implying the office of chairman.

Figure 8-2 is an example of an ASSOCIATIVE FIELD, which illustrates how a single word-symbol may evoke several referents.

Similar fields can be set up for any number of words—"light," "head," "bull," "doctor," "summer," "religion."

It would seem that more denotation and less connotation would make for better communication, but human nature does not operate that way. Suggestion is often more tactful than direct statement; it is more polite to say that a man is "a bit careless about his facts" than to call him a "liar." Poetry would vanish if we did away with connotative and figurative language. *Simile*, the comparing of one thing to another, seems to be a part of everyone's pattern of expression. "Like a rock" immediately suggests many qualities, from the texture of an object to the nature of an individual. In the latter case, it can further be divided into complimentary or uncomplimentary: on the one hand, the person referred to might have a firm character; on the other hand, he might be bull-headed. Quite likely it was because of its connotative force that the Russian premier Joseph V. Dzhugashvili adopted the name Stalin, meaning "steel."

A word-symbol may suggest too much or too little. To a desert Bedouin, the word "camel" is not an adequate symbol. He needs to know if the referent is a racing camel, a freight camel, a nursing camel, or whatever type. The same holds true for the Eskimo and the word "snow." He needs to know about the snow's texture: Is it wet, dry, grainy? Suitable for walking on? Dangerous to walk on? Just right for building an igloo? He has no single word, as we do, for "snow," but rather several words, each one different and each one including a description of the snow. As the camel is an important item in the culture of the Bedouin, so snow is an important item to the Eskimo. The importance of precise meaning in a particular word may vary from culture to culture.

Even within a culture, the particular situation in which a word is used may change its meaning, or its force, from the meaning it has in a slightly different situation. A classic example occurs in Owen Wister's *The Virginian*. The Virginian's buddy calls him affectionately a very harsh epithet, and he doesn't turn a hair. But a few moments later, when the "bad guy" calls him the same thing, the Virginian says threateningly, "When you call me that, smile!" A wife may call her husband "pittie pie," or something equally ridiculous, in their bedroom, and he grins with delight; but if she calls him the same thing in the presence of his male friends, he frowns with anger.

The meaning of a word or expression is very much a matter of context. Ferdinand de Saussure emphasized over and over that the linguistic sign is arbitrary, that the symbol is not to be confused with the thing symbolized. As Humpty Dumpty tells Alice: "When I use a word, it means just what I choose it to mean." Like Humpty Dumpty, we make the word mean what we want it to mean. Americans frequently become very irritated by the Russians' use of words like "democratic," yet the Russians are just as sincere in their application of the word to themselves as are Americans. The difference is a matter of context; the Russians do not conceive of a meaning for the term outside their communistic, or socialistic, government. As Stuart Chase says, "The true meaning of a word is to be found by observing what a man does with it, not what he says about it."

Language and Understanding

A language characteristic which acts as a barrier to clear communication is ambiguity, which occurs when a word has more than one interpretation. We saw in the chapter on grammar how a surface structure can have an ambiguous, or double, meaning. If a man says to his wife, "I'm going to visit a sick friend," the meaning is clear. But if he says, "I'm going to visit an old friend," the statement is ambiguous. We don't know if the friend is old in years, or if he and the husband have been friends since childhood. The French clarify such statements by placing the adjective before or after the noun:

un *vieux ami* = a friend of long standing
un *ami vieux* = a friend old in years

In German, word ambiguity is often clarified by the use of a different article, as:

der See = the lake
die See = the sea

To check a word's separate meanings, Ludwig Wittgenstein, a twentieth-century philosopher deeply concerned with words and their exact meanings, devised the technique of substitution. One of his examples:

Twice two *is* four.
The rose *is* red.

The verb "is" has a different meaning in each structure. This is proved by substituting the verb "equals" for "is":

Twice two *equals* four.
The rose *equals* red.

The verb "equals" may be substituted in the first, but not in the second; the second structure is clearly ungrammatical.

Economy—the tendency to use the simplest form of an expression—figures largely in many of our seemingly ambiguous utterances. For instance, the service-station attendant may comment: "You're leaking oil." Taken absolutely literally, such a statement would be shocking, if not downright offensive. However, given the context—the automobile, the technician, the service station—the driver of the car has no difficulty in decoding this message. It is much briefer than saying: "Your automobile is leaking oil from the engine."

Semantics is concerned not only with meaning and change in meaning, but also with the manipulation of meaning. Honesty in advertising, for example, is a problem which the federal government has concerned itself with. As consumers, we are warned to look closely at what the labels on products *really* say; as insurance clients we are warned to "read the fine print."

Advertising is a science, based on human responses to visual or auditory stimuli in the form of symbols. It has been shown in repeated tests that the native speaker does not actually listen to large segments of spoken language; he picks up the message by listening to key syllables, words, and phrases. (This is one reason why, to the foreigner, the speaker seems to be speaking so rapidly. The foreigner is straining to hear *every* word.)

Twenty-five centuries ago Confucius stated that when words are misused, nothing can be on a sound footing. Only when men know what names stand for, and then act as the definitions indicate, can there be true social order. Morality cannot exist apart from precision of thought and speech. To Confucius, morality and social order were virtually synonymous. Today, election years are a good time to observe the various interpretations, misinterpretations, and reinterpretations of what candidates say on issues. A news reporter may quote certain words and phrases out of context, completely changing the intention of the speaker. Or the speaker may deliberately give certain words a force they don't deserve. One political writer has complained about politicians' use of the word "free": "free" education, "free" lunches, "free" medical services. This writer maintains that there is no such thing as "free" within a society. Everything costs somebody something.

Professional conferences, labor discussions, contract-signings, all call for preliminary agreement on terms. Terms must be made precise. Lawyers make fortunes by finding loopholes in the language of contracts, agreements, and laws.

Another deliberate effort to confuse meaning is CIRCUM-LOCUTION (when statements are made in indirect, often long-winded utterances). Circumlocution may also result from a certain pomposity on the part of the speaker, or from his desire to avoid compromising himself. Politicians are particularly adept at this technique. When Robert McNamara was Secretary of Defense, he was asked if a recent build-up in American military activity in Vietnam did not constitute escalation. "Not at all," the Secretary replied. "It is merely an incremental adjustment to meet a new stimulus level." And when China and the United

States finally began to recognize each other again in the early 1970s, they moved cautiously for fear one would feel the other was warming up too rapidly. So they agreed to establish "liaison offices" rather than admit what in fact the "offices" actually were—embassies.

Circumlocution is also known as "gobbledegook." An example comes from the Department of Health, Education and Welfare, where a study was planned to determine why children fall off tricycles. The title of the study: "The Evaluation and Parameterization of Stability and Safety Performance Characteristics of Two- and Three-Wheeled Vehicular Toys for Riding."

Somewhat akin to circumlocution is PROLIXITY, or tedious wordiness, a speech characteristic which may certainly be listed among barriers to clear communication. The Weather Bureau is about as representative as any other agency when it comes to prolixity. Instead of simply saying, "It rained heavily in X County last evening," the weatherman comes out with, "A considerable amount of precipitation occurred in the region of X County last evening."

On the international level, PROPAGANDA is an effort to shape opinion through a presentation of particular views. Interestingly enough, in many countries "propaganda" is not a bad word, but in America it carries a bad connotation. Americans feel that propaganda is a method of twisting the meaning of language and of pushing untruths. In other countries, it is merely the dissemination of a particular viewpoint, a perfectly legitimate practice. If you want to get another viewpoint, read another newspaper. Certain words and phrases are easily recognizable as belonging to the more warlike lexicons of propaganda. Russia and China have constantly called America "imperialist." Yet America has observed through the years the intervention of Russia in Czechoslovakia, Hungary, East Germany, and other non-Russian countries; and China's adventure in Tibet can hardly be called anything but imperialistic.

Communication at the international level is also made more difficult by the necessity for translation. Translation involves not only finding word counterparts in another language, but also contriving ways of representing concepts when the words for the concepts are lacking in the other language. In 1962, Norman Cousins, the long-time editor of *Saturday Review*, went to Russia as an emissary of the Pope and of President John Kennedy. His purpose was to discuss international peace with Nikita Khrushchev. Mindful both of the importance of his mission and of the chances of linguistic confusion when speaking through an interpreter, Cousins spent five hours with the interpreter the evening before his meeting with Khrushchev, rehearsing his statements and making sure that the interpreter had a complete understanding *in Russian* of the critical statements to be made. According to Cousins, it turned out there were at least three dozen terms whose precise equivalents are lacking in the Russian language. But by developing different contexts for the idea he was trying to convey, he and the interpreter worked out satisfactory substitutes.

Language and Ideas

The study of the relationship between language and perception—and behavior—is called PSYCHOLINGUISTICS. Emile Durkheim, a turn-of-the-century sociologist, considered language to be a social function which exerts considerable control over the speaker. That is, a person's language is a social instrument, passed on to him by the culture in which he is raised. His language does not merely project his thoughts; it helps to form them. Some years later Edward Sapir also suggested that language is the mold of thought, that our thinking is regulated by our language. With the language that we inherit from our community, we also receive, prepacked, a set of interpretations of the things we see and hear and otherwise experience.

One of Sapir's students at Yale was Benjamin Lee Whorf, an unusual personality who had become deeply involved in linguistics. To him linguistics meant the quest for meaning. Taking off from Sapir's comments on the constraints of language upon thought and experience, he developed what has become popularly known as the SAPIR-WHORF hypothesis, or, more accurately, the principle of LINGUISTIC RELATIVITY, which relates thought and conduct to language. Scorned by some current investigators, praised by others, this hypothesis is still very much alive.

Whorf formed his hypothesis mainly out of his research in the Hopi language. The urge to systematize and classify seems to be a universal trait in man. Naturally, people have used their own language to put labels on all observable phenomena. Whorf noticed that Hopi is entirely different from what he called the "standard average European" (SAE) languages. Since linguistic items classify ideas, he felt that he had a map of the greatly different ideas of the Hopi. From an analysis of several Hopi verb forms that specify many slightly different motions of vibration, Whorf concluded that by the existence of these verb forms and their constant use, the Hopi is forced to observe the separate motions which they describe. That is to say, the Hopi actually sees—because the Hopi's language conditions him to see—certain motions that the SAE fails to see.

Some time-and-space concepts of the SAE are absent from the Hopi language; thus, in effect, they do not exist for the Hopi. For the same reason, their concepts of time and space are incomprehensible to or do not exist for SAE people. The Hopi have verbs which indicate objectively actual happenings: what can be observed at the present time, or what has been observed in the past. The concepts of time and space are combined in their verbs which indicate happenings in the past at varied distances from the speaker. That is, an event which took place at a far distance from the speaker is verbalized as something which occurred a long time in the past. The shorter the distance of the event, the more recent in time it becomes. Anything which the SAE speaker would put definitely in future time, the Hopi puts into a subjective set of verbs that includes not only an indefinite indication of the future, but also hope, expectation, anything and everything that we would consider as psychological, or, as the Hopi say, "existing in the heart." And not only in the heart of the Hopi; the set of verbs also implies the heart of all nature, all living things, all existing natural things from mountains to the Great Spirit. Such a mentality, or world view, is what causes the Indian to say that he lives more in harmony with nature than does the white man.

One method of verifying the principle of linguistic relativity has been the color test. Several linguists worked out practical schemes by which the ''codability'' or recognition levels of particular colors may be determined. They operated on the premise that the more accurately a color can be *named* in a particular language, the more accurately it can be *recognized*. English speakers can name and distinguish between yellow and orange, two easily recognizable colors in English. But when the tests were given to monolingual Zuñis, they could not make a distinction between the two colors. No separate lexical labels distinguish the two colors in Zuñi, and they did not ''see'' the difference. Navajos, too, have a color symbolization scheme which differs from that of the SAE. For them, the spectrum from green through blue to purple is all included under the single symbol *tootl²izh*. So as far as color perception is concerned, it would seem that the Sapir-Whorf hypothesis works.

But there are arguments against the hypothesis. For example, it has been found that Navajos, like some other Indian groups, have verb forms which vary according to the shape of the object involved in the discussion. If a Navajo child holds a ball in his hand, the verb form he uses reflects a round object; if he holds a stick in his hand, the verb form changes to reflect the shape of the stick; and so on. In a test, a group of young Navajo children were matched with a group of English-speaking children of the same age. It was found that the Navajo children were more adept at sorting objects according to shape than the non-Indian children. Does this prove the hypothesis that language forms condition the child to perceive shapes better? Not according to some psycholinguists; in other tests, groups of English-speaking children have come out with the same level of proficiency in sorting objects as the Navajos. Probably this proficiency was a result of having been brought up from babyhood surrounded with toys of all shapes. Experience, these linguists say, not language, makes for shape recognition.

As far as one language not having an exact word counterpart in another language, does that really mean that the concept of that particular word is also missing? Some Spanish speakers say that English has no exact translation for *simpático*. "Sympathetic" is not *precisely* the same thing. Does that mean that for the native English speaker, the concept or feeling of *simpático* does not exist? What the American has three ways of saying—"I eat; I am eating; I do eat"—the Frenchman expresses in a single locution: *je mange*. Does that mean the Frenchman lacks the concept of progressive and emphatic action? Is there something semantically lacking in the English speaker who puts the single article "the" in front of "father," "mother," and "water" alike, while the German says *der Vater*, *die Mutter*, and *das Wasser*? Is it not possible that when the Frenchman speaks of the *ambiance* of a particular restaurant and the American refers to its "atmosphere," they both mean precisely the same thing? Although the Eskimo has a number of words for snow and the English speaker but one, the American ski buff manages to communicate the quality of the snow to other skiers. And while the Chinese makes no distinction between "he" and "she" in his spoken language, like all other people the Chinese is obviously aware of the difference between males and females.

The greetings of different cultures, viewed in their original meanings, indicate different concerns. The Arabic *Salaam* means "peace"; the English "Hello" originated in "Healthy be thou"; the Vietnamese *ăn cồm chửa* literally means something like "Have you eaten rice?" All these greetings originated in a basic concern for another person's well-being, although one greeting is spiritual and the other two have to do with physical health and the condition of the stomach. We can safely assume that nowadays when the Arab, the Vietnamese, and the American give these greetings, all three have in mind essentially the same philosophical attitude. When one American greets another with "How are you?" he doesn't really expect the other to take the time to go into a detailed discussion of his physical, emotional, and financial condition.

As a friendly joke, some students in a southwestern university began to greet their bilingual, Spanish-American classmates with, "What's happening?" At first the Spanish speakers were confused. The literal interpretation of *Qué pasa?* had not occurred to them, either in English or in Spanish. It is a formalized greeting and, as such, it is distinct from its original meaning.

There are, of course, words and expressions which cannot be literally translated into other languages and still make sense. In fact, when such expressions are pulled apart word by word, they don't make much sense even in their original language. These expressions are known as IDIOMS. When a Mexican cowboy wants to take a short nap, he says: *Tengo ganas de echar un sueñecito*, literally, "I have a desire to throw a little sleep." In response to "Thank you very much," the Frenchman replies, *Il n'y a pas de quoi*, literally, "There is no what." The English formal acknowledgment of an introduction—"How do you do?" —doesn't make a lot of sense, either.

We do not know exactly what differences in thought and attitude may exist in various cultures, nor to what degree such thoughts and attitudes may be controlled or affected by the language. What can be learned from the multilingual person is still to be fully explored. While MULTILINGUALISM is defined differently by different investigators, we generally think of it as the ability to function with equal facility in two or more languages. A person learning another language is expanding or changing his environment, adjusting to different situations verbally, adopting verbal symbols to bring about that adjustment. The more skillfully the adjustments are made, the more skillfully the learner controls the new language. The multilingual person already has control of two or more languages, and presumably he functions psychologically in all of them. To a certain extent at least, his feelings and attitudes adjust to whatever language he is using at the moment. When a reasonable number of such people can be tested under rigorously controlled conditions, we will know much more about the influence of different languages on thought and feeling. A good beginning in this direction has been made by encouraging American Indian students to become linguists, so that they will be able to look at their own culture as well as other cultures from an analytic, comparative viewpoint.

Language and Emotion

The psychological force of word-symbols within a given language is well known. Everyone is aware of emotionally loaded words and phrases, particularly as they have to do with religion, sex, genealogy, cultural background, and the like. There is little logic to these labels, but they still pack an emotional wallop. To call an American a "swine" will probably just draw a startled look from him, but to call him a "pig" will produce a violent reaction. To call him a "dog" might even carry a flattering connotation, but to call him a "son of a bitch"—which is logically the same thing—will elicit a totally different response.

Of course, the attitude toward certain words varies greatly among subcultures, represented by dialects within a particular language community. A word or phrase may carry a powerful psychological impact in one dialect group, but may be considered quite bland in another. Much of the casual, everyday vocabulary of the current black dialect is inadmissible in the general white middle-class society of America. However, that situation might be changed within a few years.

Content analysis is taught to some extent in many freshman courses in composition. Words and phrases are categorized as "loaded" or "neutral." There is also a spectrum of emotional impact in such terms, ranging from favorable through neutral to unfavorable. A policeman may be called "guardian of the law" or "protector of the peace"; he may be called "policeman" or "police officer"; he may be called "cop," "flatfoot," "pig." The favorable, neutral, and unfavorable epithets are obvious. Of course, other labels are applied equally well; S. I.

Hayakawa uses "snarl-words" and "purr-words." A "purr-word" would be the feline term a husband uses endearingly when he calls his wife a kitten; a "snarl-word" would be the feline term he uses angrily when he calls her a cat.

The greatest danger in meaning classification and value judgment lies in the application of a two-valued system. This is the "black-white" categorization, with no gray area between. It's the "you're either for me or against me" attitude, expressed verbally. Alfred Korzybski, considered by most to be the father of modern semantics, reacted strongly to the Aristotelian system of dichotomizing, or splitting down the middle. According to Aristotle's law of the excluded middle, everything is A or not-A. In a democracy, a multivalued system is an imperative. Yet the Aristotelian system continues to be applied: you are a Democrat or a non-Democrat; a Jew or a non-Jew; an Indian or a non-Indian; a golfer or a non-golfer. Or as the Black Panthers have expressed it: "If you're not part of the solution, you're part of the problem." This same categorization works by association: if you mix 7-Up with good bourbon, you're absolutely hopeless; if you voted for So-and-So for President, same thing; and so on and so on.

The emotional aspects of language are a powerful factor in communication and meaning. As we have seen, sometimes words and phrases may obscure the very message they are intended to convey. Likewise, the personality of the writer or speaker may affect his intended message. The advent of TV has made public figures, from entertainers to politicians, more self-conscious than ever about their projected "image." The defeat of Nixon by Kennedy in the 1960 presidential campaign has even been attributed to the difference in their images via TV; political platforms and logic had only a minor influence on the outcome of the election. To what degree this is true is beside the point; the point is that TV did have a considerable effect.

Accents, too, work in strange ways to impede the message; regional accents may turn off listeners from a part of the country where the accent is different, yet the foreign accent of a speaker from another country may intrigue those same listeners. I once sat with some of my students through an hour's lecture by a visiting lecturer who was an Englishman. The gist of what he had to say was absolutely contrary to the beliefs of one of my students; yet I watched her from time to time and saw complete adoration on her face. When it was over, I teased her about liking what the Englishman had said. "I don't know *what* he said," she sighed blissfully. "I just love a British accent."

Some time ago Jacques Barzun cautioned students about being overly affected by speakers' peculiarities, to listen to the message instead. But perhaps Marshall McLuhan was right when he declared that the medium itself is the message. The medium could be either a TV system or a speaker.

Claims have been made, and are still being made, about the inherent superiority of a particular language for a particular purpose. Thus, German has been called the language of science, French the language of diplomacy, Italian the language of love, and so on. Such claims are little more than ridiculous. Languages and the speakers of languages have always managed to find words and phrases to express their needs and thoughts. And even if they have to borrow from another language, that still doesn't grant any superiority to the language borrowed from.

However, there has always been a certain resistance at the national level to such borrowing. In the Renaissance, certain Englishmen objected to borrowing terms from nonnative sources. They objected to such terms as "lunatic" and "prophet" and "balcony," words which are now securely a part of the English vocabulary. During World War II, it was patriotic for Germans to "purify" their language of all non-German words and expressions, and for Italians to throw out non-Italian adoptions. More recently there has been a reaction in France over the development of "Franglais," which has introduced into the French language such expressions as *le snack-bar, le boss,* and *le supermarket.* French youngsters enjoy *le dancing* at *le club.* "Spanglish" is spoken by young Spanish-Americans of the Southwest. They *parqué el carro* and *vamos a la movie.* Even in Mexico, a boy will ask a girl: *Quieres un raide?* ("Would you like a ride?"). And in the Mexican business world, management will have a *mitin* with the *boicot líder* in an attempt to persuade him to call off the boycott. Americans now "blitz" exams in colleges and buy "bonsai" orange trees for the patio. Japanese businessmen have *kakuteirus* (cocktails) with their *garu-furendos* (girlfriends), or go to a *beisaboru gamu*. Young Germans *hitchhiken* and *babysitten*, while their industrial fathers develop *brandneu Beiproducts*. It would be next to impossible to stop these borrowings. They are enrichments of the various languages, and are necessary for communication in the modern world. As far as any danger of overborrowing is concerned, languages, like water, tend to seek their own level. That is, they borrow and create and change within the bounds of communication. When the process begins to result in confusion, it slows down.

Old Meanings and New

Except from a grammatical standpoint, Modern English can hardly be called English at all. Over half the vocabulary can be traced to Greek and Latin. Beginning with the Norman Conquest, thousands of new words, mainly French and Latin, swelled the English vocabulary. This was necessary because the Old English vocabulary did not contain words for the developing sciences and arts. With the Renaissance, over ten thousand new words, borrowed from more than fifty different languages, further increased the English vocabulary. Although a few individuals have protested over the centuries, on the whole English speakers have never hesitated to borrow and adopt words from any source to fit new concepts or other needs. Even when new words are coined, as likely as not they will be put together from classical roots. "Astronaut," for example, was formed from Greek *astron* ("star") and Greek *nautes* ("sailor"). Before space flights we had the automobile: Greek *autos* ("self") and Latin *mobilis* ("moveable").

We have already described the constant changes within a particular language, changes not only in the shape of words, but also in their meaning. Literature students often find that in reading Shakespeare they have more difficulty with seemingly familiar words than with those that are totally unfamiliar. "Humour" does not mean a comical quality, but rather a psychological condition. (We still say a person is in "a bad humor.") When Hamlet comments that his uncle Claudius is "less than kind," he means the usurper of his father's throne is unnatural in his cruelty. In *Othello*, Brabantio charges Roderigo with "malicious bravery." "Bravery" in this sense means bullying or hell-raising. And when, in the same scene, Brabantio learns that his daughter, Desdemona, has eloped, he exclaims: "Oh, unhappy girl!"—meaning "unlucky" girl.

Going back to the fourteenth century we find that "nice" means "foolish." A "buxom" girl does not mean one well endowed with physical attributes; it means one who is obedient. A "hussy" is a perfectly honorable housewife (*hūswif*). And "starve" does not mean to die from hunger, but simply to die. In Old English literature, "lewd" has nothing to do with sexual obscenity, but merely describes an uneducated person. "Play" (*plegian*) may mean either to play or to fight. In adventure stories we still use the words "swordplay" and "gunplay." Old English *lastword* means not the winning of an argument, but the fame that lives on after a person's death. A phrase from the Old English poem "The Whale" indicates a rather startling change in meaning:

cymeð wynsum stenc
(comes a delightful fragrance)

A scanning of *The Oxford English Dictionary* gives a broad view of the astonishing changes in meaning that words and phrases in English have gone through during the centuries. In fact, even a good desk dictionary gives a sufficient set of examples.

Nor are several centuries required to effect such changes. We have already noted the general invalidation of the rule that created an arbitrary distinction between the use of "shall" and "will." Fries has pointed out that the rules for "shall" and "will" did not gain widespread currency until the nineteenth century. Yet the separate functions of the two auxiliaries still hold true in certain interrogative sentences. For instance, the native speaker of English senses a strong difference between "Shall we sit down?" and "Will we sit down?"

A moment's reflection will call to mind many changes occurring right now. The following example from spoken English involves a shift in form but not in meaning; perhaps the shift will carry over into written English as well. Logically, the expression of indifference "I *couldn't* care less" is correct; yet many otherwise well-educated speakers, hearing the expression far more frequently than they see it written, fail to hear the negating morpheme "-n't." So they express it, "I *could* care less." Though in grammatical—and logical—shape the two expressions are opposite, in philosophical and psychological context they carry precisely the same meaning. The same conditions cause many students to write in their themes, "I should *of* known better." More tuned to the auditory form than to the visual, they hear the abbreviated auxiliary "'ve" as "of." In normal speech, they are phonetically the same: [əv].

A current shift in meaning but not in form is represented in the changing nature of the verb "to scan." Earlier it meant to examine thoroughly, to analyze. But now it's generally used in the sense of looking over hastily. Quite likely, this more recent meaning results from the similarity of "scan" and "skim." We find that usually an underlying association causes such a change in meaning.

The sciences and professions provide new words and new meanings to the everyday vocabulary. Many psychological terms, formerly restricted to professionals in the field, are now tossed around by everyone from college freshmen to nightclub comedians. "Schizoid," "psychosomatic," "hyperkinetic" roll off the tongue as easily as "headache" and "insomnia." The space-exploration program has added words to the vocabulary of every seven-year-old who watches TV. Youngsters talk casually about "blast-offs," "countdowns," "rockets," "modules," and "space stations."

Slang is responsible for part of our language change, though just how much it would be hard to say. As teenagers are quick to point out, nothing is deader than last year's slang. Who today uses "straight" as a slang term for something very good, like a pretty girl or a flashy car? Or "drip" for an undesirable person? However, some slang words and expressions catch on and become absorbed into standard language. People who object to the introduction of slang terms into the accepted vocabulary might be surprised to learn that much of their own "standard" language was the slang of yesteryear. Two quite respectable words of today, "snob" and "sham," were slang words in the eighteenth century. So was "joke." Slang is generally thought of as a jargon of youth, originating in the need for an "in"-group identification as far as peers are concerned, and in the desire to flout authority—that is, "correct grammar"—as far as the older generation is concerned. It also represents a fresh imagination, a creativeness, and probably these qualities are what contribute most to the stimulation of the existing language. By its very newness, slang has a vigor which is often lacking in older expressions. Probably this is why, on occasion, the President of the United States will use a slang expression to make a forceful point.

While we can accept the Neogrammarians' insistence on inevitable change in language, we can now see that such change is not a blind, mechanical operation, but the result of very human social interaction.

FOR FURTHER READING

Brown, Roger, *Words and Things*. New York: Free Press, 1958.

Chafe, Wallace L., *Meaning and the Structure of Language*. Chicago: University of Chicago Press, 1970.

Chase, Stuart, *Power of Words*. New York: Harcourt Brace Jovanovich, 1954.

Cousins, Norman, "The Improbable Triumvirate: Khrushchev, Kennedy, and Pope John," *Saturday Review* (October 30, 1971). Pp. 24–35.

Deese, James, *Psycholinguistics*. Boston: Allyn and Bacon, 1970.

Hayakawa, S. I., *Language in Thought and Action*, 3rd ed. New York: Harcourt Brace Jovanovich, 1972.

Jespersen, Otto, *Growth and Structure of the English Language*. Garden City, N.Y.: Doubleday, 1938.

The Oxford English Dictionary.

Saporta, Sol, and J. Bastian, eds., *Psycholinguistics: A Book of Readings*. New York: Holt, Rinehart and Winston, 1961.

Ullmann, Stephen, *Semantics: An Introduction to the Science of Meaning*. Oxford, England: Basil Blackwell, 1967.

III

LANGUAGE
AND MAN

Language is not primarily a means of communication but a means of communion.

R. B. LePage

9

LANGUAGE AND CULTURE

Culture has been defined as the sum of transmitted behavior patterns, arts, beliefs, institutions, and all other products of human work and thought characteristic of a community or population. These characteristics are all transmitted by language. They are not inherited through the genes. A Chinese baby taken from his parents shortly after birth and raised in a Saudi Arabian society would be, except for certain physiological characteristics, the same as all the other children born and raised in that society.

Language, Culture, and Society

Ethnocentricity, or the belief in the superiority of one's own ethnic group, is manifested in the very names some groups have given themselves. The majority of the American Indian tribal names, when translated into English, mean something like "original people." The Navajo's name for himself is *Dené*, "man" or "people." *Jemes*, the name of a Pueblo tribe, also translates into "the men." So does the root *ntu* of *Bantu*. *Ainu*, the name of the non-Japanese people of Hokkaido, means "human being." In still other cultures, ethnocentrism is maintained through mythology and religious rites. Practically every culture has a creation myth, with itself as the first created people.

A common language is the strongest cement for holding together a cultural group. No case is known of either a language or a culture existing without the other. Obviously, no language would survive in isolation, and civilization needs language to transcend time and transmit itself. Culture and language are so tightly related that they may be considered as parts of the same thing. We have already observed how language changes over time and place; so does culture. Cultural changes tend to occur along with language changes, and then the two proceed to reinforce each other. As proto-Indo-European dialects changed over the centuries into different languages, the cultures represented by those languages likewise became differentiated. Separating from a common linguistic ancestor, Russian culture, German culture, and Italian culture are today markedly different in many areas. Even within an individual speech community, changes in cultural attitudes are revealed in language. Such changes can be observed from one generation to the next: words that were taboo in one era, particularly concerning such subjects as sex and religion, become commonplace in another.

Strong identification with a cultural group seems to be an inherent necessity of man. The hermit is the exception. A person consciously or unconsciously moderates his own individualistic drives in order to maintain acceptance within his social organization. What is acceptable socially is "moral"; what is unacceptable is "immoral." In some cultures, the codes of social acceptance are written down; in others, they are passed on orally. The culture as a whole tends to be more conservative, or resistant to change, than the individual. Consequently, there is always tension between the individual and his social group. To meet environmental changes, a certain degree of inventiveness and change is necessary in each society. The inventive individual, however, must moderate his language and his actions to remain within the outer limits of his culture's elasticity. If his behavior, linguistic or otherwise, becomes too radical, then he may be cast out of the group. He may be killed, he may be exiled, or he may simply be ostracized. The last—being cut off from communication with his cultural fellows—may be as severe as the first two.

Societies and Groups

As we have just noted, tension is created when an individual within a group deviates from the behavioral—including linguistic —patterns of acceptance. Another source of tension is the so-called generation gap, referred to in Chapter 3. This particular tension seems to be an inherent part of human society. It is recorded in the Bible and in even older writings. In Egyptian hieroglyphic records of the Middle Kingdom (c. 2000 B.C.), the "Schoolboy Maxims" carry the parental admonition:

> I am told that you forsake studies and give yourself up to pleasures . . . that you love books less than beer. Therefore give heed, you naughty one, you obstinate one, who will not hear when you are spoken to.

At mid-twentieth century, Rogers and Hammerstein included the problem in their delightful musical comedy *Flower Drum*

Song. Members of both generations sang: "What are we going to do about the other generation?" "We don't even speak the same language" is a complaint voiced by parents in many cultures; the implication is strong that the whole value system, including the linguistic, is being upset if not destroyed by the younger generation. There seems to be no record, however, of one generation completely changing the language of a speech community, in spite of the supposed breakdown in communication.

Another tension is created in a cultural group, or linguistic community, by warfare, particularly when the community is invaded. The original Celtic-speaking Britons were virtually exterminated by the fifth-century invasions of Angles, Saxons, and Jutes. Celtic remained in varying degrees in Wales, Scotland, and Ireland, but in England proper the Germanic speech supplanted the Celtic. The community speech became what we know today as Old English. The next overpowering invasion, the Norman Conquest of 1066, changed the language tremendously, but did not eliminate it. The conquering Norman baron ate "pork" at his table, but the conquered Anglo-Saxon servant tended "swine" in the yard. For a while, there was a very real breakdown in communication, but eventually Middle English developed as the national language, although with very distinct dialect variations.

Still another source of tension is immigration, and the United States is probably the clearest example of that tension today. In the early days of the American republic, *assimilation*,[1] or the adoption by a minority group of the cultural characteristics of the majority, was an expected process. The early immigrants came to America for better economic standards and greater opportunities for their children, yet these first-generation, foreign-born newcomers still felt a terrific wrench at the loss or erosion of their native culture. They felt an especially great loss in watching their children grow up and away from the parental

[1] This definition of *assimilation* should not be confused with the purely linguistic one given in Chapter 4.

language. These dynamics continue today. On the streets of New York and in the barrios of New Mexico, one can see and hear parents speaking to their children in Spanish and the children replying in English.

The loss of a native language, or of contact with members of that language group, is a sort of loss of identity, at least until the new language, together with the new culture, has been adopted. Second-generation children are eager to blend into the peer group, and if they are surrounded by native speakers of, say, English, they quickly and easily switch to English. For the youngster this is a simple and painless process, but for the parents it can be a painful one. When grandchildren arrive, the elders may have difficulty communicating with their grandchildren, and the loss of the original culture seems certain. In the more fortunate immigrant communities, the younger generations continue to speak the language of their elders in the home, while in the "outside world" they speak English. They are, in effect, bilingual.

Assimilation does not always proceed smoothly; in fact, it sometimes does not proceed at all. To deny a man his native tongue is to deny him his culture, his identity, and this he will resist. In India, as well as in Canada, Belgium, and other countries, riots have erupted largely over the question of language. Britain took Canada from France by force of arms in 1763, but more than two hundred years later over 60 percent of the people of Quebec still speak only French, while hardly a quarter are bilingual in French and English. In Belgium, a long and bitter struggle over language finally ended in a compromise. The Flemings of the north speak Dutch, while the Walloons of the south speak French. The Flemings were unwilling for their children to be educated in French, so in 1971, to end the bitter, often violent language battle, the government passed laws granting the Flemings autonomy in language, cultural affairs, and education.

Hawaii offers an example of how different cultural groups can work together to overcome linguistic barriers. In Hawaii, the modern youngster is frequently trilingual. If his ancestry is mainly Japanese, he may speak Japanese to his grandparents, Standard English in school, and Hawaiian Pidgin among his fellow students (see p. 53). PIDGIN is a reduced language, and not really the native language of any who originate its use, although it may become the first language for succeeding generations, in which case it should properly be called CREOLE.[1] In the settling of Hawaii, the newcomers—Chinese, Japanese, Filipino, Spanish, English, Danish, and others—in order to communicate with each other and the native Hawaiians, developed a mixed, structurally simplified language drawn from several of their languages. Such pidgin languages have developed all over the world, mainly through commerce. The word "pidgin" itself is a corruption of the word "business."

Of particular interest to dialectologists and educators in the United States today is Black English, which we discussed in Chapter 3. It is the English spoken by a large proportion of black Americans. This dialect has been traced to a creolized form of English based upon a pidgin spoken by slaves along the West Coast of Africa, and in the Americas and the Caribbean Islands. Many black Americans are bidialectal—they can function with equal facility in both Black English and Standard English.

Modern industry, among other forces, demands constant shifting of the labor population. As a result, family and community ties are often broken, and sometimes the individual succumbs to *anomie*, a sense of alienation and disorganization which generally results in delinquency and other antisocial behavior. On the Mainland of the United States, anomie is a serious problem which must be confronted and reckoned with by the government and by various social services. Hawaii, however, a group of close-set islands far from the Mainland, and thus more conducive to strong family and community ties, has perhaps not suffered the tensions introduced by different languages and different cultures as much as have other parts of the United States.

Worldwide, from South Africa to northwestern Europe,

---

[1] This is a purely linguistic definition of *creole*.

as modern societies become more industrialized, cultural dis-location increases, producing a host of problems for sociologists to analyze and governments to cope with. However, it should be noted that bilingualism or multilingualism is not a problem in itself, as long as other stabilizing factors are present, such as the family and the homogeneous community. In Switzerland, youngsters speak two, three, or more languages effortlessly, yet retain a strong sense of identity. It is the cultural values them-selves which cause misunderstanding and unfriendliness when one group finds itself a minority within a larger society. In the southwestern United States, for example, the fatalism of the Mexican-Americans often comes into conflict with the social values of the "Anglos," as the members of the majority culture are called. The Mexican-American didn't get drunk because he drank too much at a party; he got drunk because too much liquor was served. And if he breaks a bottle, he says, "I let it fall and it broke itself." Nor does he "miss the bus"; he says, "The bus left me." Such statements the Anglo interprets as reflecting a lack of responsibility rather than a deep-seated fatalism.

Language and Government

At the government level, the question presents itself of how much cultural diversity—and autonomy—may exist within a nation without threatening the strength of that nation. Con-sidering the small fraction of man's existence on earth which has been spent in social groups of more than a few hundred people, the concept of nationalism is a fairly recent one, yet, a major one.

Readily available international air travel and the invention of satellite communication have created a world in which no country is isolated from, or unaffected by, others. And nations are highly competitive. Japan is the classic example of how national prosperity is proportional to national unity. Military security, too, depends upon unity of purpose as well as armaments.

We have noted that a common language is the cement of unity. Recent history provides any number of examples of how the problem of national unity has been coped with by various powers, and to what varying degrees of success. As long as the Bolsheviks in Russia were a militant, revolutionary group, they approved of autonomy for the dozens of minorities under the czarist rule— the Uzbeks, the Yakuts, the Letts, the Mongols, and others. This meant these diverse peoples were to be free to function in their own separate languages and to follow their own cultural aspirations. However, after the overthrow of the Czar and the takeover by the Soviet government, the official attitude changed. Beginning with the third stage of the Russian Revolution, about 1934, there was a strong revival of militarism and nationalism. Cultural minorities in Russia have ever since been steadily pressured into nationalistic uniformity. In other countries, however, minorities are still being exploited by Communist agitators for revolutionary purposes. Lenin said in 1921, in his *Thesis on Tactics*:

> In countries whose population contains national minorities, it is the duty of the Party to devote the necessary attention to propaganda and agitation among the proletarian strata of these minorities. The propaganda and agitation must, of course, be conducted in the languages of the respective national minorities. (From Eugene H. Methvin, *The Riot Makers*. New Rochelle, N.Y.: Arlington House, 1970. P. 139.)

In India in 1951, it was reckoned that 845 different languages and dialects were spoken. After India's post-World War II change from colonial status to independent nation, her officials recognized that to achieve political and economic independence, unity of purpose would have to be encouraged through a sense of nationalism. And this could only be brought about by effective communication. The Union Government designated Hindi as the official language, but it happened that out of a population of nearly half a billion, less than one-third spoke Hindi. Then the government, practically enough, designated the fourteen major languages of the country as the official languages of India. But even that did not provide a sufficient basis of communication. So, since the great majority of the educated people, the leaders, spoke English, that language became the official government language for as long as necessary; that is, until the people could be educated to Hindi.

Language, Culture, and Education

Formerly, the various cultural minorities in the United States have provided their own ways of culture retention, including language training. Greek-American children have been taught their parental language by the Greek priests; Jews have been taught Hebrew in the same way; Hungarian and German communities have continued many cultural customs, including the use of their native languages, so that the children of these communities have grown up practically bilingual. Now, however, through equal-opportunity legislation passed by Congress in the last decade, such language training has been made a responsibility of the federal government. And in certain instances, the value of teaching Standard English has been called into question, on the grounds that imposing Standard English through the schools is just another form of political and cultural oppression.

Bilingual training for minority youngsters in the elementary grades is another matter. Every year hundreds of thousands of five- and six-year-olds enter American schools unable to speak English at all. Thousands of others speak only nonstandard dialects of English, which means they are handicapped in communication at the standard level. In order to give these youngsters an equal opportunity linguistically, programs have been established to teach the students in their native tongues as well as in Standard English. The native language is psychologically deeply rooted, and concepts occur in it spontaneously. However, the elementary-school youngster is amazingly flexible, and unless hostility toward the new language is instilled in him through outside forces, he quickly and painlessly adjusts to his new bilingual environment. If the programs are administered and taught by well-trained professionals, the youngster masters the new language by the end of the third grade, if not before.

The same situation exists in Mexico. Great numbers of North Americans and Europeans and Orientals now live in Mexico, either permanently or on a temporary basis. Their children go to Mexican public schools, where instruction is all in Spanish. The children very quickly adjust to the new language, and speak Spanish as fluently as their Mexican classmates.

Interestingly enough, cultural chauvinism isn't the only factor in language preference. The prestige factor and the economic factor often take precedence. In the court of the Czar of Russia most of the nobility spoke French exclusively, because French was then the "elegant" language of Europe. A great many political leaders in India today have never learned Hindi. While the Vietnamese fought for decades to get the French colonials out, Saigon is still full of Vietnamese who take great pride in their fluent French. Indeed, a very large colony of Vietnamese live permanently in Paris. Three-quarters of a century after Spanish control ended in the Philippines, Spanish is still a language of influence, although federal programs have attempted to impose Tagalog as the national language to be taught in schools. In America, certain linguists and sociologists are urging the use of Black English on a par with Standard English, but the main objections usually come from the parents of black ghetto children. The parents recognize that economic advancement demands fluency in the standard dialect.

A Multicultural Society

To deny the benefits of a multicultural society would be extremely shortsighted. In fact, a monocultural society is becoming increasingly hard to find these days. Anthropologists are constantly on the lookout for such a society. Practically all the countries of Europe have been permeated by one another over the centuries. The entire Mediterranean littoral has mixed freely since time immemorial, and Arabic words make up a good bit of the Spanish language. All the countries of Western Europe have conquered one another over and over again, with the consequent mixing of cultures. The greatest benefit to come out of the bloody medieval Crusades was not religious but economic and intellectual—the result of cultural borrowing between the English and the Western Europeans and the Middle Easterners.

The United States today is an outstanding example of cross-cultural borrowing. As anthropologist Ralph Linton once pointed out, the American, from the time he drinks his coffee in the morning until he crawls under the blanket at night, is making use of material borrowings from other cultures. This is true linguistically also; the English language probably has the largest vocabulary of any language in use, and this has come about through borrowing. Mexico is another example of the blending of cultures, with a population mixture of Spanish and indigenous Indian and immigrants from all over the world: conqueror, conquered, and immigrant. The same holds true of most of the countries of Latin America. It is an age-old pattern. And we have seen already how languages are related.

On the one hand, we see a need for cultural stability for the sake of national unity, and on the other hand, a definite need for cultural change and growth in order for a nation to function in today's world society. No culture has yet attained perfection, and probably none ever will. And there is no culture that cannot stand to profit by abandoning certain of its customs or rituals, such as the ancient ritual of tossing babies into a fire in worship of Moloch, or the more recent custom of human slavery.

The problems involved in working toward harmony within a nation—and among nations—are problems for linguists, sociologists, and psychologists, as well as for political scientists. One of the greatest barriers to understanding and harmony is the placing of value judgments on speakers of other languages. "He does not talk like me, therefore he is not like me, therefore . . . ." Or, as Jim says to Huck in *Huckleberry Finn*: "Is a French-man a man?" "Yes." "Well, den, Dad blame it, why doan' he talk like a man?" Few if any cultures look upon themselves as inferior. We have already referred to ethnocentricity as it is manifested linguistically.

Linguistic distinctions are even used for purposes of warfare. SHIBBOLETH, a password to distinguish one linguistic group from another, was used in early biblical times. The Gileadites, in battle with the Ephraimites, used the Hebrew word for "ear of corn" as a password because their enemy could not pronounce the initial "sh." The Ephraimites said, "Sibboleth," and were killed. Such shibboleths were used by GI's against Japanese soldiers in World War II. Japanese seeking to infiltrate American lines under cover of darkness were challenged with words and phrases containing many "l's" and "r's," phonemes which generally gave them trouble, no matter how well they spoke English.

Of course, chauvinism isn't the only reason we sometimes hesitate to learn and adopt other languages. Another language may "sound funny" to us; therefore, we feel embarrassed when we attempt those "funny sounds." Small children ordinarily do not feel self-conscious; they like to make all sorts of sounds. Consequently, they pick up other languages just as readily as they learn other skills. Certain forms of etiquette may also interfere with learning another language. For instance, a polite Japanese female will never stick out her tongue, and the more traditional ones still cover their mouths when smiling, to keep from exposing their teeth. So, when they attempt to learn the English "th" by sticking out their tongues, they go through quite a bit of embarrassment.

A number of factors may contribute to a feeling of resentment between speakers of different dialects within a country. For the speaker of one dialect to adopt the other's dialectal characteristics may be viewed as selling out to the enemy. For example, the American Civil War, which ended more than a century ago, left feelings of hostility between the North and the South that even today show up in attitudes toward extreme regional accents. The Northerner may associate the Southerner's drawling intonation, dropping of final consonants, and "you all" with laziness and stupidity; while to the Southerner, the

Northerner's more clipped intonation, harsher pronunciation, and the use of the plural "youse" may sound like a movie gangster. Fortunately, with increased education and the mobility of our modern population, such feelings of antagonism are becoming rarer.

All over the world, for both social and economic reasons, value judgments are made on dialect variations—judgments that place greater value on certain cultural characteristics. A young woman from Liverpool wishing to work as a stewardess for British Airways must abandon her Lancashire accent and dialect while working, and cultivate the Received Standard English, which is based upon the dialect spoken at Oxford and Cambridge. A Japanese may identify—and judge—other Japanese by their regional speech patterns: Tokyo = sophisticated; Kyoto = cultured; Osaka = commercial. Some years ago a young American woman from the South became a movie actress and was immediately given intensive speech training to eradicate her Southern accent. In her first major role, she was cast as a Southern belle, and had to learn her original speech patterns all over again. For awhile, radio and TV newscasters were trained in what was then considered a neutral General American dialect, but in recent years more individuality has been allowed in their speech patterns. Social and regional dialects used to be the source of a great deal of comedy, but at present this is a very touchy practice. What may seem funny to some strikes others as cruel ridicule.

Interference in communication is aggravated by a hyper-critical judgment of accents and of other speech characteristics. The late Mary Colum, wife of the Irish poet Padraic Colum and a prominent literary critic in her own right, once complained bitterly to a young graduate student in her class at Columbia University that she couldn't understand what he was trying to say because of his accent. The student had a rather pronounced Southern accent. With more honesty than Southern chivalry, he retorted that he was having an equally difficult time getting through her Irish brogue. As a rule, people who are primarily concerned with *what* another person is saying, rather than with *how* he is saying it, have less difficulty than do people who have the opposite concern. Two specialists at an international conference—say a Japanese doctor and a German doctor—using English as a lingua franca, may have strong pronunciation difficulties but will understand one another quite well because they are exchanging information, not silently commenting on each other's poor English. In fact, just because of their desire to cooperate, they may have less difficulty in understanding each other than two people from different regions of the same country.

It is to be hoped that the modern linguistic approach to education will reduce ill will arising from language and dialect differences. On the other hand, it is readily seen that the more standardized a common language is, the easier communication becomes.

FOR FURTHER READING

Dasgupta, Jyotirindra, *Language Conflict and National Development: Group Politics and National Language in India.* Berkeley: University of California Press, 1970.

Fishman, Joshua, *Readings in the Sociology of Language.* New York: Humanities Press, 1968.

Florida FL Reporter, Vol. 7, No. 1 (Spring–Summer, 1969).

Hall, Robert A., Jr., *Pidgin and Creole Languages.* Ithaca, N.Y.: Cornell University Press, 1966.

Kroeber, A. L., *Anthropology: Culture Patterns and Processes.* New York: Harcourt Brace Jovanovich, 1963.

Landar, Herbert, *Language and Culture.* New York: Oxford University Press, 1966.

LePage, R. B., *The National Language Question: Linguistic Problems of Newly Independent States.* London: Oxford University Press, 1964.

Madsen, William, *The Mexican-Americans of South Texas.* New York: Holt, Rinehart and Winston, 1964.

O'Neil, Wayne, "The Politics of Bidialectalism," *College English*, Vol. 33 (January 1972). Pp. 433–38.

Rice, Frank A., ed., *A Study of the Role of Second Languages in Asia, Africa, and Latin America*. Washington, D.C.: Center for Applied Linguistics, 1962.

Smith, Alfred G., ed., *Communication and Culture*. New York: Holt, Rinehart and Winston, 1966.

Speech is the best show man puts on.
Benjamin Lee Whorf

IO

SPEECH AND LANGUAGE ACQUISITION

How Babies Learn Their Language

Animals have their systems of communication transmitted genetically from generation to gene ation. The young bee communicates with its fellow bees in the unchanging, stereotyped system that bees have always used. It does not have to learn the system; it is born with it. A newborn puppy, removed from its mother and other dogs and raised on a bottle, would, after several years, still be able to communicate with other dogs, even though it had not in the meantime encountered others of its species.

Only the human baby must start from scratch and learn the language spoken by its parents and others in the community. A number of theories have been advanced to explain how this learning takes place. John Locke, the seventeenth-century English philosopher, believed that at birth the human mind is a *tabula rasa*, or "clean slate," waiting for impressions and experience to make their recordings there. In the eighteenth century, Herder suggested that the urge to speak was an inherent impulse. In the nineteenth century, Hermann Paul stated that a person's speech formations do not come from a memorized stock. More recently, generative-transformationalists have repeated Paul's statement, adding that the child has the *ability* to utter an infinite number of well-formed sentences that he has never heard before nor spoken before. Although certain empiricists today still believe that our linguistic system is acquired by experience, it would appear that a baby is born with the apparatus and the capacity for speech, and perhaps more.

Whether the built-in impulse to talk emerges from a specific and isolated section of the brain—a "culture-acquisition device," as it has been called by some anthropologists—or whether the capacity is a nonlocalized psychological trait exclusive to human beings, is still not known. To call the impulse complex neural equipment is about the best we can do at present. But we know it is there, and we know that it works. However, speech itself must be learned.

The processes involved in the development of language control are still a mystery. The stupid child as well as the bright one masters a complete system of complex rules underlying a language; and the child learns the system whether he is taught directly or whether he is left alone to pick it up by himself from those about him.

Children in isolation from all other human beings, though, do not spontaneously begin to speak a language. We have a number of documented cases of children raised in isolation from fellow human beings. Around the end of the eighteenth century, one of these children—Victor, the wild boy of Aveyron—was captured when he was about twelve years old. He could not talk and he behaved in every way like a wild animal. A physician tried for five years to teach him to speak, with almost no success.

Another case was in India, early in this century: two children, Kamala and Amala, were found living with wolves. They behaved like wolves, and did not speak. The younger one died before any speech-training results could be truly ascertained. The older one lived, and eventually learned to speak a few words only. Judging from such cases, as well as from recent studies in language acquisition, it appears that children must be supported in their speech development from the very beginning by constant reinforcement from parents or older children or some other human being. With attention and support, children begin to react and respond so quickly to new verbal situations that their reactions are almost instantaneous. But if their first speech (babbling) impulses are not reinforced through social support, it may be that the impulse simply dies.

A baby's very first sounds can hardly be called speech-sounds. His cries signal hunger, thirst, or some other discomfort, or they are simply a part of an instinctive testing of all his muscles and organs, including the vocal cords. No specific sounds are associated with specific needs, in spite of what fond parents and relatives may say. If they see that the baby is wet or that his bottle is empty, they may link his particular cries with the particular situation. But in controlled experiments, with mothers and others listening from behind screens to the different cries of the babies, no accurate associations could be made. Thus, even mothers can be wrong. (However, pediatricians can tell from distinctive peculiar cries if the baby has brain damage or certain other abnormalities.)

After two or three months of these organically determined cries, the baby moves into the BABBLING stage, in which his sounds signify, among other things, contentment. More important, it is in this stage that his prelinguistic sounds gradually progress to imitative sounds. Before this cognitive, or reasoning, level is reached, though, the baby has gone through an interesting phase of sound-production. The month-old baby's vocalizations consist of a ratio of nearly five vowels to one consonant, while the adult's is approximately one to one (in English). The first vowels are front vowels; the back vowels come as the baby develops physically. Consonants develop the other way: back consonants first, then front consonants. It is said that babies normally make sounds reflecting the whole range of sounds in the world's languages. An American baby may clearly sound the French trilled *r* and the German *ü*. After once making a particular sound, the baby has, in effect, opened up the vocal tract and the neural passages so that it will be easier for him to repeat that sound.

Moving toward the twelfth-month stage, the average infant takes more and more notice of the speakers around him, usually his parents. His self-stimulating babbling gives way to stimulation from the sounds of those about him, particularly when his attempted repetition of those sounds brings pleasing attention to himself. Adults will often repeat after him the sounds of the native language which the baby most closely approximates. By twelve months, his perceptive development has usually progressed to the point where he can repeat sound-patterns made by an older person. The youngster's gradual physical growth is accompanied by the equally gradual development of the speech areas of the brain. His physical speech apparatus is slowly developing too. (This development is not completed until well after the adolescent "voice change" at twelve to fourteen.) At about seventeen months, the child understands and responds to simple commands, such as "Give me that" and "Touch your nose." Competence, or comprehension, comes long before production of true speech-sounds. That is, the child usually begins to distinguish words spoken by others by the end of his babbling period.

From the twelfth-month stage until he actually learns to talk, the child is continually making a tremendous effort. Stimulated by an *echoic* tendency, he tries to repeat the sounds he hears. This echoic tendency is demonstrated first in the babbling stage, in which he echoes himself; then, as his perception becomes more acute, he echoes others—parents and older children. Another impulse at this stage is to please, because when he approximates actual language sounds, he is rewarded by smiles, exclamations of delight, and caresses. Perhaps this is one of the reasons he stops his babbling and attempts imitation of the words he hears.

On the average, then, the baby is attempting to form words by twelve months, though the interpretations of proud parents may prematurely convert such sounds as "da" to "daddy," and "ba" to "ball." Apparently his control of words, his ability to form them intelligently, and his comprehension of their meaning come about by trial and error, his success being indicated by parents' reactions. Before two years, his understandable vocabulary has increased considerably, and he can form two- and three-word locutions. To measure the actual vocabulary possessed by the developing child, and his full awareness of the meaning of each item, is rather difficult, and psychologists do not claim absolute accuracy for their results. One set of results gives less than half-a-dozen words for the one-year-old, nearly three hundred words for the same youngster at age two, and about two thousand words at age three. Again, his comprehension vocabulary is much greater than his production vocabulary—the stock of words he himself articulates. His actual production does not seem to be necessarily related to any intellectual status, although parents sometimes develop anxiety over a nontalking infant. I remember vividly one new mother bending over her baby's crib, repeating "Rhinoceros, rhinoceros, rhinoceros," with the idea in mind of making a genius out of the child. The woman's next child, born about a year and a half later, was pretty much left to himself, as far as vocabulary development was concerned. He developed verbally at just about the same rate as his older sibling.

In at least one area of speech development, it would appear that parental reinforcement might even retard the child's efforts. That is in the reinforcement of baby talk. The child's mispronunciation in his early efforts—"wa-wa" for "water," and "ki-ka" for "kitty-cat"—sound so cute, particularly to first-time parents, that they repeat the child's pronunciation, reinforcing him in his mispronunciation. This may result in ridicule for the youngster later on when he begins to play with his more clearly articulating playmates.

The young child has a perception of meaningful sound-categories and of the relation of word-symbols to their referents (see pp. 147–48) much earlier than he does of syntactical arrangement of words. In fact, in associating word-symbols with referents, he includes events as referents, too, as when he applies the word "mamagive" to his mother's feeding and cuddling him. That is, "mamagive" is a single symbol relating to the event "mama give." This stage in the child's speech development is called the HOLOPHRASTIC stage, in which this one-to-one relationship exists. Sometime after he passes his second year, he begins to recognize that his single word-symbols may be broken into parts: he learns that "mama give" and "papa give" involve manipulation of separate linguistic units, and he begins to play with the units, just as he plays with his toys. This is the ANALYTIC stage. He experiments, putting together his units and testing them on his listeners, usually his parents. He might say, "Doggie bite daddy," or "Daddy bite doggie," convincing his parents that they are raising an incorrigible liar, unless they realize that he is just learning the flexibility of language; he is not concerned with truth. A strain of this sort of testing carries an impishness that could be labeled the "Dennis the Menace" syndrome. As he grows older, he might repeat words and phrases which he has heard, in order to check the effect on his parents. They might be revelations of ill-timed truth, like "You got a big nose," to the visiting rich uncle; or they might be incredibly vulgar expressions he has overheard someone else use, convincing the parents that their incorrigible liar is also a moral degenerate. The semantic impact has not yet touched the child; he is still in the trial-and-error stage of learning the language.

The average child does not do much with verbs in his developing sentences until he is about three years old. His memory increases tremendously after this age, so that he is able to retain words and phrases, and is able, too, to turn out longer locutions of increasing complexity. He experiments by analogy, particularly with verbs, as when he says, "The bird flied in the tree," and "The cat runned under the house."

It is often said that the child has internalized his native language by the time he is six years old. That is, he has developed an intuitive knowledge of the grammatical rules by which he can both form acceptable sentences he has never used before and understand sentences he has never heard before. The fact is, however, that in the normal human being the learning process never ceases. Most definitely, the individual's vocabulary continues to increase as long as he moves about in society. A book, a new friend, a change in profession, any of these factors or any number of others will contribute to an increase in vocabulary. Furthermore, any English teacher can testify that many high school students—and even college students—have not acquired a very firm command of their native grammar. And professional writers constantly experiment with different grammatical forms as well as with purely stylistic ones. We can say, with more accuracy, that language-learning processes decrease tremendously by the time of adolescence. This is one reason why—another generalization—youngsters learn another language more easily than older people. But this generalization scants the fact that the child, from babyhood on, works extremely hard to master the native language so that he can fit into the life about him. Language learning is not easy. Fortunately for the developing youngster, he is not actually aware that in learning his native language he is the hardest worker in his family.

Learning Another Language

In many ways the learning of a second language parallels the learning of a first language—that is, if we consider learning a language as gaining a working mastery of it in speech and comprehension. Prior to World War II, most high schools and many colleges considered learning a language as gaining a reading knowledge of it. A conversational mastery of the language was seldom attained. Many of us labored through two years of high school Latin, painfully translating Caesar's *Commentaries on the*

Gallic War, and perhaps getting into Cicero. French and Spanish fared about the same. Often taught by a teacher who would probably have been unable to order a meal in a restaurant in France, we sweated through a simplified version of *Les Trois Mousquetaires* and maybe some Victor Hugo. Our first culture shock came when we went overseas in World War II and discovered, in our attempts to communicate with native French speakers, that nothing that D'Artagnan ever said to Milady de Winter seemed to be appropriate to the present situation. Suddenly, the most important men in the various military outfits were sons of immigrants, able to speak Italian, or French, or German.

Crash programs were set up by the government to train people to *speak* other languages, and not just the standard French, German, and Spanish, but also the heretofore "exotic" languages, such as Chinese, Japanese, Russian, Arabic, and a dozen or so others that most Americans had never even heard of. The method was severe: instead of the three-hours-a-week routine of high school and college, the language trainees at the Army language school in Monterey were exposed to drill in the target language six to eight hours a day. Many dropped out of the programs, unable to survive the brainwashing effects of the rigorous routine. Those who did survive came out at the end of six or eight weeks speaking such English-related languages as French, German, Spanish, and Italian with working fluency; non-English-related languages took a year or more.

The Army drilled the trainees in the DIRECT method, based on the principle that a child masters his own language by hearing, then speaking, then possibly reading and writing. The trainees started out by listening to short phrases in the target language, spoken by a native speaker. They repeated the phrases after the instructor in class, and again in tape laboratories. They used the MIM-MEM technique (mimic-memorize) to master lists of phrases that are particularly helpful in general conversation, and PATTERN PRACTICE to memorize the grammatical system. Always the emphasis was on phrase structure, not on single vocabulary items. In this way, the trainees picked up and internalized the native rhythm, the intonation patterns of the target language.

One of the many reasons that children learn another language more easily than adults do is that children don't suffer from embarrassment at making funny, unfamiliar sounds (see Chapter 9). The aim of the direct method is to constantly expose the learner to the sounds and rhythms of the target language, thus gradually clearing away the "strangeness" of it. The method also provides a means of instant correction by the teacher, so that the student doesn't internalize an incorrect pronunciation or grammatical structure. For example, the learner of French is drilled in the separate pronunciations of *dessous*, pronounced /dəsu/ ("below"), and *dessus*, pronounced /dəsy/ ("above").[1] The phoneme /y/ does not exist in the inventory of many Americans, and is only used by others in such words as "news," pronounced by some as [nyz] and by others as [nuz]. Even more difficult is the Arabic velar fricative /ɣ/, the soft gargling sound that babies make so easily, American babies as well as Arab babies.

Language is a habit, and must be internalized to the degree that it operates as a reflex. A general greeting and response is just such a reflex. An English speaker, hearing "Hello. How are you?" replies almost without thinking, "Fine, thanks. And you?" In foreign-language learning, greetings and useful questions like "How much is this?" "What is this called?" and "Where is the restaurant?" are practiced over and over until they are "overlearned." That is, they become reflexes. This is the mim-mem technique.

Pattern practice moves from the simple to the complex, just as the youngster does in mastering his own language. This technique includes what are called "minimal steps," as well as the standard correction and reinforcement practices of other methods. For example, in a simple question-and-answer pattern —"What is this?" "It's a book"—the minimal step would be to change only the substantive, to fill in for "book." In reply to

[1] Tables 5-1 and 5-3 give the equivalents of the phonetic symbols used here.

the next "What is this?" the response might be: "It's a desk,"
or, "It's a pen." Only one item in the entire pattern is changed
at any one time, at least in the beginning. Innumerable variations
may be contrived for the patterned substitution drill, with the
gradual substitution of more than one item at a time. One
effective pattern is cued by the instructor as follows:

> INSTRUCTOR: John is going to the movies. Bill.
> STUDENTS: Bill is going to the movies.
> INS: Helen.
> STU: Helen is going to the movies.
> INS: You.
> STU: You are going to the movies.
> INS: We.
> STU: We are going to the movies.
> INS: I.
> STU: I am going to the movies.

This drill provides a good bit of practice in subject-verb agreement.

These same techniques are valid no matter what the target
language is—English or Urdu or Apache. Specialists in materials
preparation and in teaching techniques have pretty well determined the tolerance for drill of the average person or the average
class—that is, just how long students can continue to drill in a
particular exercise before a change of pace is necessary. A great
deal of the early stages is more concerned with imitation than
with understanding, but the latter cannot be ignored. People
learning another language, particularly older people or more
sophisticated students, want to know just what it is they're
saying. A resistance is immediately evoked when the instructor
orders: "Never mind what it means; just repeat it after me."

As the student progresses, the materials should reflect
cultural relevance. Spanish-American youngsters learning English
in bilingual classes in New Mexico learn the names of animals
with which they're already familiar: coyotes, squirrels, jack-
rabbits, and hawks. The story has been told of a missionary-
linguist who tried to teach the Lord's Prayer to his Eskimo

congregation, but sensed that the English words weren't really getting across to the Eskimos. By a fortunate insight, he substituted "fish" for "bread"—"Give us this day our daily fish"—and the meaning became relevant to the congregation.

Even as the students attain enough facility in the target language to be able to read it and write it, they should still be regularly drilled in speech. The degree of fluency is almost entirely a personal matter. A student who is highly motivated to speak with native fluency may eventually reach that stage. Other persons may prefer to keep their "foreign" accents. Foreign movie stars in America have often deliberately retained their French or Spanish or German accents as trademarks, for economic reasons. Other individuals have a fear of losing their cultural identity if they become truly bilingual (see Chapter 9). Actually, this fear is somewhat justified, since to completely adopt another language is to adopt another culture as well. Consequently, some members of minority groups in the United States today are confronted by a painful dilemma. A minority member wishing to move into the majority group either socially or economically, or for whatever reason, recognizes that in order to do this he must master the majority dialect. But in doing so, he may discover that his membership in the original group is being modified. If a hostility exists between the two cultural groups, a feeling of anomie may disturb the now-bilingual person. On the other hand, if a favorable relationship exists between the two cultures, the bilingual may enjoy a tremendous ego lift and be truly enriched psychologically and intellectually.

FOR FURTHER READING

Bar-Adon, Aaron, and Werner F. Leopold, *Child Language: A Book of Readings*. Englewood Cliffs, N.J.: Prentice-Hall, 1970.
"Brain," *Encyclopaedia Britannica*.
Brown, Roger, *Words and Things*. New York: Free Press, 1958.

Carroll, John B., *Language and Thought*. Englewood Cliffs, N.J.: Prentice-Hall, 1964.

Lado, Robert, *Language Teaching: A Scientific Approach*. New York: McGraw-Hill, 1964.

Miller, George A., *Language and Communication*. New York: McGraw-Hill, 1963.

Smith, Frank, and George A. Miller, eds., *The Genesis of Language: A Psycholinguistic Approach*. Cambridge: M.I.T. Press, 1966.

Show me your image in some antique book,
Since mind at first in character was done.

Shakespeare

If we didn't have writing, we wouldn't have mis-
spelled words.

A student

II

WRITING

The Earliest Writing

It might seem a bit strange that language as speech is
common to all peoples, but writing, the graphic representation
of speech, is relatively rare. The vast majority of the thousands
of languages and dialects that have served mankind's needs have
never been recorded. If speech is a system of arbitrary symbols,
varying from language to language, writing is even more arbitrary
and artificial. Like language, its origins are concealed in the
mists of the past, although considerably more is known about
the earliest forms of writing than about the earliest forms of
speech. For writing is a visible record not only of man's history,
but of itself as a graphic artifact.

Our modern industrial societies could hardly exist without written records. However, that doesn't mean that tightly organized societies cannot exist without writing. In fact, in at least one well-developed society, writing was at first looked upon more as a hindrance than a help. According to an ancient Egyptian legend, when Thoth, the ibis-headed god of wisdom, revealed to King Thamos the art of writing, the king saw it as a drawback to learning and to civilization. He complained that children and youths, who had formerly applied themselves diligently to memorizing the orally transmitted wisdom of the past, would, with written records, neglect to exercise their memories. Undoubtedly, other men of old recognized the plasticity of a child's mind and his capability for maintaining the oral traditions of his culture.

The myth of Thoth as the divine giver of the art of writing is more or less duplicated in other cultures. Cadmus, the culture hero and legendary founder of Thebes, is supposed to have brought writing to Greece from the East (Cadmus < Semitic *qédem* = "man from the East"). Similarly, Itzamna, direct descendant of the goddess of the dawn, brought hieroglyphs to the Mayas from the East. In China, a number of culture heroes are credited with bringing writing to the people. Two of them, Fu-Hsi and Tsang-Ke, are supposed to have conceived of written characters after studying the designs of cracks which formed in heated tortoise shells, a device for fortunetelling in ancient China. Whether writing came to China in the third or fourth millennium B.C.—or even earlier—is not presently known.

The early Egyptians, as much as any people, stressed the supernatural and mysterious nature of writing. HIEROGLYPHS (Greek *hieros* = "sacred or supernatural," and *glyphe* = "carving") were the sole province of the holy ones, comprising king, priest, and scribe. At first the hieroglyphs were "thought-pictures," appearing to a holy one in a dream, a message from a god. This magical quality of a written word or symbolic drawing is in a prehistoric tradition, dating back to our caveman ancestors, who drew pictures of game animals on the walls of their caves in order to invoke magical powers to help them in the hunt.

Runes, the ancient Germanic symbols for writing, were originally devised for magical purposes.

The expression of magic was not the only purpose of primitive writing; early peoples also drew pictures or carved on bark or stones simply to convey messages. They cut notches in sticks and tied knots in strings to tally counts or for other records. Some American Indian tribes used notched sticks, knotted strings, and even picture-symbols drawn on skins for sending messages. Before their invention of written characters, the ancient Chinese also used knotted strings. Although inscribed symbols were associated with magic, they were also developed for the less romantic purpose of commerce. As trade developed and increased among tribes of diverse languages, these tribes needed a means of sending messages and of keeping records. The ''Mediterranean Signary,'' a collection of vases and fragments from prehistoric tombs in Egypt, the Sinai Peninsula, and Spain, bear about three hundred different mercantile symbols. This collection has been tentatively dated as far back as 5000 B.C. The symbols have proved to be related to proto-Sinaitic writing.

The first writing symbols, as far as we know at present, were PICTOGRAPHS, which represented literally an object, but not an entire scene, as did the prehistoric cave paintings. To the ancient Chinese, the pictograph ⌂⌂⌂ symbolized ''mountain,'' just as the same hieroglyph did to the ancient Egyptians. (For our purpose, *pictograph* and *hieroglyph* will mean the same thing.) The symbol ⊙., from the more primitive ✳ , represented ''sun'' to the Chinese and the Egyptians alike. The similarity between the earliest Chinese symbols and the earliest Egyptian symbols is apparent; they were both pictographs. Disregarding the mythical origin of Chinese writing, its actual beginning is not known. Egyptian hieroglyphs, however, are believed to be derived from the pictographs of the Sumerians, a rather mysterious nation of non-Semitic people who first inhabited the Mesopotamian region in the fifth millennium B.C., or even earlier. Whether they came from the north (they are not thought to be of Indo-European stock) or whether they were aboriginals from nearby is not known. Since the earliest Egyptian hieroglyphs date from before 3000 B.C., the Sumerians must have been writing considerably earlier. Some authorities have even placed hieroglyphs as early as 5000 B.C.

The next step in the development of writing occurred when pictographs were stylized into IDEOGRAPHS, or, to use a more approved term, LOGOGRAPHS (Greek *logos* = "word"; *graphein* = "to write"). That is, the inscription came to symbolize the word, or the idea of the word, rather than the literal object itself. With the passage of time, such symbols became more abstract both in shape and in meaning. The Egyptian symbol for "lion" came to mean not just the animal, but the idea of supremacy. The symbol for "hall" connoted "counsel," because wise men consulted in a hall. The stylization of form came about gradually; one of the reasons probably was that more people were learning to read and write, and so a greater uniformity of symbols was needed. For early Chinese scribes, who used a brush stroke, straight lines were easier and simpler to make than were the circles and other shapes in the original pictographs. So the pictograph ⊙ , "sun," became the logograph 日 , and the pictograph ⌁ , "mountain," became the logograph 山 .

With little modification, the modern Chinese still uses the classical logographs. The uniformity of the symbols makes understanding possible among Chinese speakers of totally different languages. A Chinese from Shanghai, a speaker of Mandarin, may be unable to speak with a waiter in a Cantonese restaurant, but he can read the menu and write out his order. Both men use the same writing system, whose symbols are not phonetic. Through the centuries, the Japanese, Vietnamese, and Koreans also borrowed Chinese calligraphy, so that scholars in all these countries can read and write the same literature, although they may not necessarily be able to speak with each other.

In the Mesopotamian region, CUNEIFORM writing developed, changing the shape of the pictographic symbols, much as did Chinese brush stroke writing. The Middle Eastern scribes worked on tablets of soft, wet clay, using a stylus that produced a wedge-shaped mark (Latin *cuneus* = "wedge"). The clay tablets were then baked to hardness in ovens. The formalized logographs "straightened out" the rounded figures of the earlier pictographs. Figure 11-1 illustrates the shift in form of the pictograph for "bird" to the cuneiform logograph.

FIGURE 11-1

From Pictographs to Cuneiform Writing

Pictograph	Sumerian Cuneiform	Babylonian Cuneiform	Assyrian Cuneiform

The oldest cuneiform writings in existence were discovered around the middle of the nineteenth century. Consisting of several clay tablets, many of them fragments, they were in the ruins of royal libraries at Nineveh and Ur and other ancient Sumerian and Assyrian cities. The tablets date back as far as the third millennium B.C. They carry prebiblical accounts of the Great Flood, the Creation, and other mythological or legendary events. They also carry the oldest epic in writing, the myth of Gilgamesh, a Sumerian king. This epic is an elaborately constructed poem with a strong rhythm, stock epithets, and other literary devices that characterize the *Iliad*, *Beowulf*, and other sophisticated epics.

Syllabic Writing

Like the slow, often imperceptible change in language itself, the change in writing from pictographic to logographic to SYLLABIC was gradual. The first logographic symbols had no phonetic significance, but the Sumerian scribes became aware of the phonetic quality of the largely monosyllabic words in their language. They particularly noticed that sometimes two words, or syllables, had the same pronunciation, but different meanings; such words are called HOMOPHONES ("similar sounds"). In English, "sun" and "son" sound alike; the same symbol might be employed to represent both. In Sumerian, the words "arrow" and "life," both pronounced *ti*, were homophones, so an early scribe used the symbol 𐀴 or ⋙ to represent the sound of *ti*. To illustrate again in English: if we were to represent the sound /rid/[1] syllabically, we might use the symbol of a reed: ⬛ . Then, in writing, we would use the same symbol to represent a man's name, "Mr. Reid," or the verb "read," or the noun "reed." Youngsters sometimes play code games using such just a syllabary. They code the word "belief" syllabically as a bee, ✿, + (plus) a leaf, ✿

The Akkadians, a Semitic people who inhabited Mesopotamia, rapidly adapted to a partially syllabic style of writing, too, as did the Egyptians. Whether these Middle Eastern peoples borrowed each step from one another, or whether they developed their systems similarly as a matter of course, is not known. It was probably a combination of the two. Anyway, by 2500 B.C., syllabic writing was combining with logographic writing, though not entirely displacing it. The Egyptians continued to carve their hieroglyphs in stones as late as 100 B.C.; but with the development of papyrus as a flexible writing material, they gradually progressed through a cursive stage called *hieratic* (also from *hieros*, "sacred") to the even more fluid *demotic* (Greek *demos* = "common people") system, a combination of hieroglyphic and syllabic in which the symbols are joined together, as in our modern handwriting. Figure 11-2 illustrates the shift from the more literal logograph for *ankh*, "life," to the hieratic and demotic characters.

Perhaps as a result of the change in writing during this time, the following period, known as the Middle Kingdom (c. 2100–1600 B.C.), is considered Egypt's classical era of literature. It was during the classical period that *Sinuhe, the*

---

[1] See Table 5-1 for the pronunciation of the phonetic symbol used here.

FIGURE 11-2

Egyptian Writing

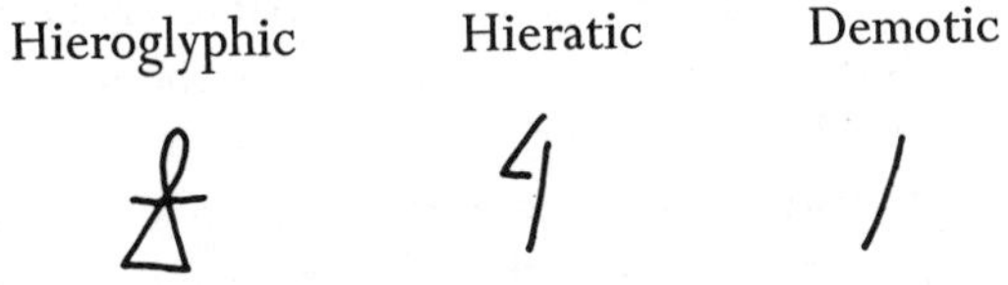

Hieroglyphic   Hieratic   Demotic

Egyptian was written, fragments of which are still preserved in papyrus manuscript. In our own era this story was rewritten and made into a movie.

A Cherokee Indian syllabary was devised in the early nineteenth century by Sequoyah and used by missionaries and the Indians themselves. It is based largely on Latin letters. In Latin America, however, Mayan writing, still not completely deciphered, was developed long before the Spanish conquest brought Latin letters to the New World. This writing is thought to have phonetic value.

The Japanese today use a syllabary system of writing. By the sixth century A.D., they had begun to adapt the Chinese logographs to Japanese sound values. These symbols, forty-eight of them, are called *kana*, and each symbol represents a syllable sound. For example, one symbol, 　 , represents not a letter but the syllable *ka*; 　 represents the syllable *na*; 　 is *su*; 　 is *ro*; and so on. The educated Japanese still read and use the classical Chinese characters, but among the general populace the more cursive, or flowing, syllabic writing is predominant. Koreans, too, have made similar syllabic adaptations for their written language. Vietnamese adopted the Western alphabet centuries ago.

Alphabetic Writing

It appears that a considerable mixing of different cultures is instrumental in the development of writing systems. As trade and warfare continued among the various Semitic peoples of the Middle East, writing advanced more toward phonetic representation, finally evolving into the ALPHABETIC system. From pictures of an object or an event, to symbols of syllable-phonetic values, written characters eventually became strictly phonetic. The first examples of alphabetic writing were found in Sinai and have been dated variously from 2500 B.C. to 2000 B.C. Inspired by the Egyptian demotic writing, the western Semites reduced the unwieldy system of symbols to a few dozen signs—called the West Semitic Syllabary—each of which was given the value of a consonant. (Modern Arabic is still written with letters for consonants only.) By 1500 B.C. the Semitic alphabet seems to have been fully developed.

The Phoenicians, those enterprising traders and middlemen, then adopted and modified this primitive alphabet and proceeded to spread it throughout the Mediterranean border countries. The contribution of the Phoenicians—Semites themselves—was to give names to the graphic signs that had evolved from the early pictograms. Figure 11-3 shows what the development was like.

FIGURE 11-3

From Hieroglyph to Alphabet

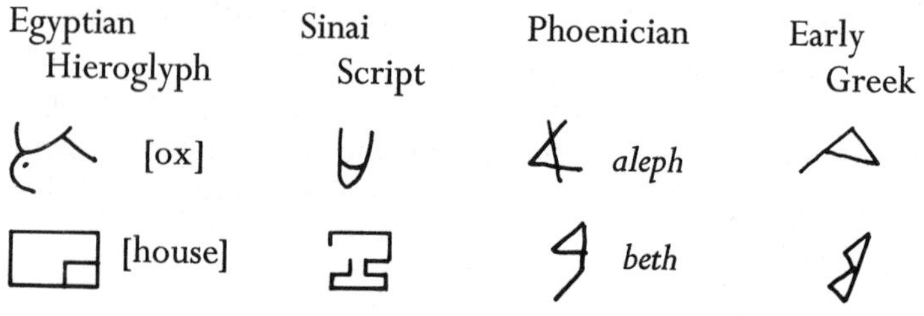

Egyptian Hieroglyph	Sinai Script	Phoenician	Early Greek
[ox]		aleph	
[house]		beth	

Around the first millennium B.C., the Phoenician alphabet came to the Greeks of Asia Minor. The Greeks reshaped, renamed, and added symbols to the collection they had thus acquired, developing the first true alphabet, the ancestor of the alphabets of many modern languages, including English. If the earlier Semitic, as well as the later Phoenician, writings have also been called alphabetic, then what is the difference between their symbols and the Greeks'? The difference is that the Semitic symbols were still somewhat syllabic; that is, each symbol represented a consonant with a vowel understood, as in modern Arabic. For example, the word for "man" in Arabic is written with three consonant characters: *r-j-l*, pronounced "rajul." The main contribution of the Greeks was to add symbols for vowels.

The Greeks further separated any pictographic significance from the name of the symbol. As seen in Figure 11-3, the Phoenician alphabetic symbols themselves derived from pictographs, and were named for the referents they symbolized. The names were ACROPHONIC (Greek *akros* = "topmost," and *phone* = "sound")—that is, the sound of the name represented the sound of the letter. (For example, in Modern English, the letter "B" is pronounced "bee.") The Phoenicians had given names appropriate to the symbols that were originally represented pictorially. The Greeks adopted—and adapted—some of the names for the symbols; but in the case of the Greeks, *alpha* is meaningless. It does not mean "ox" or anything else. Nor does *beta* mean "house." (The two names put together give us "alphabet.") They are simply acrophonic, as is the modern American name for "Z": "zee," or in British English, "zed."

The transition from Phoenician to Greek is shown in Figure 11-4.

The Romans probably got the alphabet from the Greeks by way of the Etruscans, who possibly got it directly from the Greeks in Asia Minor before they—the Etruscans—migrated to northern Italy. The Romans, of course, adapted the alphabet to their own spoken language.

The order and direction of early writing was sometimes vague. Some writing went from right to left, some from left to right, and some was *boustrophedonic* (Greek *bous* = "ox," and *strephein* = "to turn")—that is, the lines alternated between

FIGURE 11-4

Two Early Alphabets

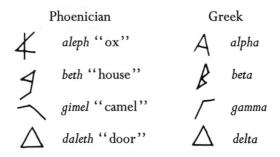

	Phoenician		Greek
	aleph "ox"	A	*alpha*
	beth "house"		*beta*
	gimel "camel"		*gamma*
	daleth "door"		*delta*

right to left and left to right, like an ox plowing a field. The earliest Latin writing, about the fifth or sixth century B.C., is from right to left. Arabic writing, a right-to-left script, developed from a form of Aramaic. Aramaic derived from Phoenician, as did Latin, however indirectly. Therefore, Arabic writing is distantly related to Latinate writing. However, there seems to be little or no resemblance between modern Arabic writing and, say, modern English writing. Some authorities date the earliest Arabic writing from the ninth century B.C., others from the fifth century B.C. The Arabic greeting, *Al-salaam alaykum*, illustrates the right-to-left writing. :

السلام عليكم

alaykum   salaam   al
be upon you / peace / the

For awhile it seemed that perhaps the dating generally accepted for the development and transmission of the alphabet might be discredited by the discovery of Linear B (see p. 67). This writing was first discovered in mid-twentieth century in Crete on tablets found in the ruins of a palace which had been destroyed by fire at the end of the fifteenth century B.C. Other tablets bearing the same script were later found in Pylos, and others later yet in Thebes, north of Athens. The script was finally deciphered in 1952. It was found to be closely related to the later forms of Greek. While certain of the symbols were isolated as vowels, Linear B turned out to be mainly a syllabic rather than an alphabetic system. As in the case of the Mediterranean Signary (see p. 201), the symbols of Linear B are mainly mercantile. While the decipherment of this script has answered many questions about early Greek dialects and the development of the alphabet, it has raised other questions which are still to be answered.

About the time that the Linear B tablets were being written in Crete and Mycenae, the Brahmins of India were writing their sacred scripts in symbols borrowed from the West Semitic Syllabary. Called DEVANAGARI (Sanskrit *deva* = "god," and *nagari* = "of the city"), it was used to write down the *Vedas*, the oldest literary texts preserved in an Indo-European language. Devanagari is mainly syllabic, with separate symbols for vowels in initial position. A faint resemblance to the Phoenician and early Greek symbols may be noted in the first two letters (compare these letters with those in Figure 11-3):

a   b

Another, and related, alphabetic system mentioned earlier in this chapter was the RUNIC. The system was devised at first for purposes of magic (Gothic *runa* = "secret, mystery"); the magical powers of runic characters were still recognized as late as the seventeenth century, and people were burned to death by Christians for displaying the symbols. Interestingly enough, *runo* also carries the meaning of "incantation" in Finnish, a non-Indo-European language. According to Norse mythology, runes were a gift from Odin, father of gods, and himself the god of wisdom and poetry. Like other early writing symbols, the Germanic letters were angular, which made it easy to inscribe them on metal, wood, and bone. Runes were formerly thought to have come directly from the Latin and/or Greek alphabets; more recent scholarship indicates that the runic characters, and probably the phonetic concept, came from a version of the early Greek alphabet, by way of the Etruscans, who had migrated from Asia Minor to northern Italy. Germanic tribes penetrating the northern Alps may have become acquainted with the Etruscans and their inscriptions as early as the fourth century B.C. If this is true, then runes are related to, but not descended from, the Latin-Greek alphabet. Undoubtedly, some of the symbols had been devised by tribal magicians before the encounter with the Etruscans, and these symbols also became part of the runic alphabet. Another interesting correspondence, though undoubtedly coincidental, is that of the Sumerian syllabic symbol ↑, which represented the Sumerian god Enlil, and the runic symbol ↑, which represented Tiw, the Norse god of war. By about 200 B.C., the entire Germanic community was sharing a common runic alphabet, of twenty-four letters, called the *futhark*, from the first six letters:

A Look at Writing in England

Although the runic alphabet was acrophonic and perfectly adjusted to ordinary writing, still it was probably used more for magical purposes than for literary purposes when it was brought from the Germanic lands in the fifth century A.D. to England. When St. Augustine came to England in 597, bringing Christianity, he also brought with him the clerical Latin of his day. The Latin alphabet became the writing medium of England, though the form of some of the letters was gradually modified by Irish penmanship and the Celtic version of the Roman alphabet. Runic writing did not disappear, however, with the acceptance of Christianity in Britain. On the contrary, it reached its highest artistic form in the eighth century, when part of the religious story called *The Dream of the Rood* was carved in runes on the Ruthwell Cross in Dumfriesshire in the Scottish Lowlands.

Since every language differs from every other, adjustments and modifications had to be made to adapt the Roman alphabet to the sounds of Old English. The Romans did not have the sound "th" as in "theater," a word they took from the Greeks, so instead of borrowing the Greek letter θ (theta), they improvised the digraph "th." The Anglo-Saxon scribes then borrowed the "th" from the Latin alphabet, for English had both the voiced and the voiceless sounds, /ð/ and /θ/ (see Table 5-3). But many readers confused the "th" with plain "t," so the scribes borrowed two symbols from their stock of runes, voiceless þ (thorn) and voiced ð (eth) (see p. 61). That should have solved the problem, but it didn't. Scribes began to use the two letters interchangeably, sometimes spelling "that" as ðæt and sometimes as þæt. It was not till about 1400 that the digraph "th" was reintroduced into English.

One other rune that the Anglo-Saxon scribes adopted was þ (wynn). The Latin alphabet showed "v" for the "w" sound. Caesar's famous boast, "I came, I saw, I conquered," was written *Veni, vidi, vici.* The Anglo-Saxon scribes at first used "u" and "uu" to indicate "w." But the situation became so confusing that they adopted þ, a symbol used until the Norman conquerors replaced it with double-u for "w." Here is a line from Caedmon's Hymn, comparing the early version with the later version:

uerc Uuldurfadur, sue he uundra gihuaes
weorc Wulderfæder, swa he wundra gehwæs

(work of the Glory-Father, when he of wonder each)

An amusing blunder in attempting to reconstruct the older forms of English occurs today in such signs as "Ye Olde Antike Shoppe," in which "Ye" is presumed to be, and pronounced as, the old personal pronoun "ye." An early spelling of "the" in Middle English employed the thorn, þ:

ine þe yeare of oure lhordes beringe, 1340

but in copying the thorn some scribes did not close the top of the letter, resulting in Þe. And even after the printing press was imported into England, printers used y to represent þ, as in a 1550 rendering of St. Matthew:

on yt dai Jesus comming from ye hous
  [þat]   [þe]

The Beginnings of Literacy

In brief, then, the development of writing throughout most of the literate world has been from pure pictorial illustration to idea symbolization to syllabic and finally phonetic representation. As we have seen, some cultures, like the Chinese and the Arabs, stopped at one stage or another. Since the concept of the phoneme, or distinct working sound, is relatively recent, those cultures which did, and still do, employ syllabic symbols have been able to function adequately. But to other peoples, it appeared unnecessarily bothersome to use over five hundred syllabic symbols when their spoken language had fewer than forty phonemes. As we have seen, the Greeks were the first to clearly separate each sound and to give it a symbol.

Originally the restricted property of a select few—mainly the priesthood—writing has spread throughout the world to become the common property of anyone who chooses to use it. The adoption of papyrus as a writing medium, undoubtedly because it was so much more portable than stone, increased the literacy in ancient Egypt. Paper was invented in China about A.D. 100, and remained in that country until the mid-eighth century, when some Chinese troops attacked the Arabs at Samarkand. The Arab commander captured some of the Chinese, who luckily were skilled in the making of paper. From then on, paper became a property of the Arabs. The Greeks imported it during the eleventh century, and when the Arabs occupied Spain in the twelfth century, they began manufacturing paper there.

Meanwhile, throughout the Middle Ages the principal writing material in Western Europe and England had been parchment and vellum, prepared from the skins of sheep, goats, and calves. Literacy was not widespread; reading and writing were generally limited to monasteries, where most of the parchments were prepared and rolled up into scrolls. Copies were made by hand, and writing became an art form, as some of the illuminated manuscripts seen in museums testify. However, this was a pitifully restricted and expensive means of recording and spreading literature of any sort, as King Alfred sadly discovered in the ninth century.

At first, paper was rejected in some of the European countries. Called "cloth parchment," it was not considered fit for official documents, because it was less durable than vellum. However, during the fifteenth century paper gradually superseded vellum. From Spain it was introduced into France and then into England, although no paper was actually manufactured in England until the late fifteenth century.

In the time of Chaucer illiteracy was still the lot of the vast majority; learning was mainly the province of the legal profession and the Church. The Black Death of 1348–50 carried off a heavy percentage of these educated people, further reducing literacy. But with the introduction of printing into England in 1476, hundreds of copies of all sorts of works were run off and distributed, and literacy grew and spread. William Caxton, one of the first English printers, helped greatly in the development of a standard English speech and a uniformity in spelling. The state of the language is described in the introduction to his translation of the *Aeneid*:

> And fayn wolde I satysfye every man, and so to doo, toke an olde boke and redde therin; and certaynly the englysshe was so rude and brood that I coude not wele understande it.

By 1640, a small flood of printed matter had appeared in English under more than twenty thousand titles, everything from huge folios, such as the First Folio of Shakespeare's works, to pamphlets and broadsides, the latter a single sheet printed on one side only. This wealth of printing, together with the spirit of the Renaissance, resulted in a tremendous upsurge of literacy. It has been estimated that from one-third to one-half of the people of Shakespeare's London could read.

Writing and Spelling

A constant problem accompanying alphabetic writing, though, is that of spelling. There is no such thing as a purely phonetic system of writing. Spoken language inevitably changes, gradually perhaps, but irresistibly. Writing—or, more properly, spelling—does not keep pace with the changes in speech, so that the spelling of a word in one age would not necessarily indicate the pronunciation of the same word in a succeeding age. In Chapter 5 we noted how certain words are no longer pronounced as they are spelled, because their spelling represents an earlier pronunciation of these words. Many highly educated people have difficulty with spelling, partly because of the lack of phonetic relationship between the written and the spoken word. One may well ask: "Why don't we change the spelling, then?"

Since early times attempts have been made at spelling reform. One of the first recorded efforts is that of Orm, a cleric who wrote in his *Ormulum*, about 1200:

> þatt mann birrþ spellenn to þe follc
> (that one befits spelling to the people)

Orm's main effort was to show more clearly the sounds which were not, he felt, indicated sufficiently in writing. By doubling those letters that represented distinct or stressed pronunciations, he hoped to bring speech and writing closer together.

Even with the spread of literacy in England, there was for centuries an extremely indifferent attitude toward spelling. For example, Lanfranc's *Science of Cirurgie*, the most influential book on surgery throughout the Middle Ages, has the word "surgery" spelled five different ways on the very first page. All the existing manuscripts of Chaucer's *Canterbury Tales* differ in spelling. Sir Walter Raleigh, the Renaissance courtier, spelled his name several ways, none of them as it is spelled here.

As bad, if not worse, were the efforts of the purists who overcorrected. In Chaucer's day, the "gh" in "light" and "night" was pronounced; even though the pronunciation has changed, the spelling has remained the same through the Renaissance and up to today. By analogy with "light" and "night," a word formerly spelled somewhat phonetically—*delit*—was corrected to "delight." A number of books were published in the 1500s for the correction and improvement of the spelling of English, but none of them won favor. Thomas Smith's *Dialogue concerning the Correct and Emended Writing of the English Language* (1568) took notice of one discrepancy still current in spelling: we have twenty-six graphemes (letters) to represent thirty-five or more phonemes, not counting pitch and stress signals, as in "súrvĕy"-"sŭrvéy" (see p. 106). Smith proposed increasing the alphabet to thirty-four letters and marking the long vowels. William Bullokar, in his *Booke at Large, for the Amendment of Orthographie for English Speech* (1580), proposed several diacritical marks for pitch, stress, and so on, in the manner of modern French, Spanish, Vietnamese, and several other languages.

Spelling reform was advocated in America by Benjamin Franklin. He talked to Noah Webster, author of the original Webster's dictionary, who at first disagreed with Franklin, but later came around to his viewpoint. To demonstrate his later ideas in spelling reform, Webster wrote in 1780:

> Every possible reezon that could ever be offered for altering the spelling of wurds, stil exists in full force; and if a gradual reform should not be made in our language, it wil proov that we are less under the influence of reezon than our ancestors.

In spite of books on spelling reform, English writing continued to be frequently individual, as witness this testimonial of an early American bourbon enthusiast:

> One Small drink would Stimulate the whole Sistom. It Brot out Kind feelings of the Heart, Made men sociable and in them days Evry Boddy invited Evry Boddy That Came to their house to partake of this hosesome Beverage.

At least, the spelling is quite phonetic.

Upon first consideration, reforming our English spelling to match current pronunciation would appear to be a very simple and desirable procedure. Learning to spell phonetically would certainly be easier for the school youngster; and the foreigner learning to read and write English would no longer be frustrated by the dissimilar pronunciations of such similar constructions as "bought," "bough," "through," "rough," and "though." On the other hand, a change in spelling often loses the original meaning of a word. The word "lady," for example, indicates nothing by its present spelling. But its original Old English form, *hlæfdige*, meant just what is spelled out: "loaf-divider," or "loaf-distributor," just as "lord" was originally *hlafweard*, "loaf-guard." And "daisy," whose original meaning is lost in its present spelling, was in Old English *dægeseage*, which literally meant "day's eye." At the present time we can look at the word "breakfast" and see that it means just what it says: "break-fast." But if it should be spelled as it is pronounced, /brɛkfəst/,[2] there would no longer be a clear etymological connection; it would just be another word to be memorized, as we must memorize, usually without association, words borrowed into the language, such as "chauffeur."

Another problem created by a drastic spelling reform would be to make practically useless all the books, magazines, and other written records now current. Changed pronunciation and spelling over the centuries have made Middle English a subject

---

[2] Table 5-1 gives the equivalents of the phonetic symbols used here.

to be studied diligently, and Old English even more so. An overnight reform of current spelling would result in the equally quick loss of the usefulness of our libraries. Schools would go out of business until the printing presses brought all knowledge up to date in the new spelling. The cost of such a project would be astronomical.

A major problem to be confronted by spelling reformers would be, *Whose* pronunciation? Although dialectal differences in the United States are generally less extreme than in many countries which are much smaller, they are still sufficiently marked as to raise this question. In a large portion of the United States, people do not pronounce "r" after a vowel or at the end of a word: "forty" is pronounced [fɔtɪ] and "four" is [foə]. This omission is also characteristic of Received Standard English, the "proper" pronunciation of English in England. And what about the intrusive "r," as in the Bostonians' pronunciation of "Cuba" ("Cuber")? What about the lack of distinction in their pronunciation of "hoarse" and "horse" that characterizes some educated speakers of English? And the similarity of "cot" and "caught" in some dialects? And what about homonyms, such as "sight," "site," "cite," and "made," "maid," and so on?

If there is to be a change, a reformed spelling, then chances are it will follow the suggestion of Noah Webster: it will be "a gradual reform." People in general are far more conservative than they like to believe. The unfamiliar is often viewed with a touch of alarm, if not with hostility. Whatever may happen to writing in the future, for the present we do not seem to be under any great pressure to simplify spelling.

FOR FURTHER READING

Budge, E. A. W., *Egyptian Writing*. London: Routledge and Kegan Paul, 1970.

Elliott, Ralph W. V., *Runes, an Introduction*. New York: Barnes and Noble, 1971.

Gallant, Roy A., *Man Must Speak*. New York: Random House, 1969.

Gelb, I. J., *A Study of Writing*, rev. ed. Chicago: University of Chicago Press, 1963.

Irwin, Keith Gordon, *Man Learns to Write*. London: Dobson Books, 1958.

Ogg, Oscar, *The 26 Letters*, rev. ed. New York: Thomas Y. Crowell, 1971.

Wemyss, Stanley, *The Languages of the World*, *Ancient and Modern*. Philadelphia: Stanley Wemyss, 1950.

For now we see as through a glass, darkly.

1 Corinthians 13:12

12

THE FUTURE OF LANGUAGE

What Languages Might Become

Speculating on the future of language is just about as chancy as speculating on its origins. We know that language changes. It would seem that in the light of our ability to reconstruct vanished languages by the comparative method, we should be able, partly by the same method, to project into the future and set up models of future languages. Probably we could set up the models, but we would have no guarantee that people would ever actually arrive at such language systems. We have no way of knowing what catastrophes—man-made, such as wars, or natural, such as tremendous earthquakes or a space collision—

might interfere with our projected languages, changing them radically.

Taking English as an example, we can reasonably guess that it will continue to simplify itself, as it has done over the past several centuries. We have seen in the preceding chapters how it has evolved from the heavily inflected system of Old English to the simpler, word-order system of Modern English. Artificial, prescriptive rules about the usage of such items as "shall" and "will" are being invalidated. Inflectional forms in pronouns, such as "who" and "whom," are being leveled out, with word order making the necessary distinction between subject and object. Like the French *C'est moi,* "It's me" sounds far more natural to the average American than "It is I." A more casual attitude toward grammatical usage permits an increasing use of contractions, such as "I'm" and "he's"; in the past, contractions were frowned upon in more formal writing. In other words, much of what goes as very informal usage today will be quite standard in the future, even in formal writing.

Probably the dwindling number of irregular verbs will dwindle even more. With "dive"-"dove"-"dove" being replaced by "dive"-"dived"-"dived," other verbs may follow suit. Just as "drip" regularized from Old English *dreap-drupon-dropen* to "drip"-"dripped"-"dripped," so might "drive" gradually regularize to "drive"-"drived"-"drived." We still read in older literature about a ship that "hove to," but that verb has been generally regularized to "heave"-"heaved"-"heaved." Two verbs which seem very much in the process of becoming one are "lie" and "lay." Even educated people consistently confuse the two in such constructions as: "I laid the book on the table" (correct); but, "I laid on the couch," and "I'm going to lay down for awhile" (questionable). The verb "lie" may possibly be used in the future only in the sense of telling an untruth.

We have observed how phonetic changes occur in languages. In English, thanks to the Great Vowel Shift (see pp. 77–78), the medial vowel of Old English *wif*, already as high and forward as it could go, diphthongized from [wif] through [wəif] to [waif].[1] Where can it go from here? Old English *nama* moved from [nɑmɑ] up to [nem]. Where will it go next? Through economy of effort, perhaps, our language has lost the velar fricative [ɣ] and trilled [R] of Old English. If we consider the same dynamic— economy of effort—and the German-inherited characteristic of stressing the initial syllable, we can predict that a word like "suggest" [səgdʒést] will gradually become [sʌ́dʒɨst].

Spelling reform has already been discussed in the preceding chapter. Although English is probably the worst language in the world when it comes to phonetic spelling, any drastic overhauling of the spelling system would create more problems than it would solve. Gradual changes, however annoyingly slow, are more practical. And they are taking place. In the seventeenth century, we spelled "work" and "town" and "shut" with a final *e*: *worke, towne, shute.* "Behavior" and "favor" were spelled with a *u* right into the twentieth century: *behaviour, favour.* (In England, they are still spelled that way.) Quite possibly the next streamlining step in spelling reform will be dropping the silent "gh" in "light," "night," "bright," and so on. These words have already been spelled "lite," "nite," "brite" in some publications and advertisements.

About vocabulary, it is even more difficult to conjecture. We can readily understand how the ancient art of alchemy was replaced by the more scientific discipline of chemistry. With the fading of alchemy many words belonging to that art became lost or obsolete. "Brimstone" and "lemaille" and "philosopher's stone" are terms that are rarely if ever used today. But who could have foreseen the sudden resurgence of interest in astrology which swept the United States in the 1960s? "This is the dawning of the age of Aquarius" proclaimed the musical play *Hair*. Fortunetelling and casting of horoscopes became popular; high school and college students and a whole crop of

---

[1] Tables 5-1 and 5-2 give the equivalents of the phonetic characters used here.

astrologers brought back to life terms which had begun to fade from general usage, such as "zodiac" and "cusp" and "house" (the last two in the astrological sense).

The earlier notion that linguistics, physics, neurology, and still other disciplines are all completely independent of each other has been replaced by a recognition of their interrelationship. Technical terms from one discipline are used in another. "Code," "signal," "feedback," "entropy," "field,""wave," "particle," "matrix," and a host of other words are used with generally the same meaning in different disciplines, including linguistics. This cross-discipline approach has opened up new horizons for all the sciences involved, and it holds much promise for the future.

The Universals of Language

A current assumption in linguistics which may have implications for both the future of language and the teaching of language is that all languages share basic common features. The earlier assumption was that languages differed from each other in innumerable and unpredictable ways. The present assumption is based partly on the belief that a child has an inherent capacity for learning any of the world's languages with equal facility. This seems to indicate that the differences between languages are only in their surface structures. Linguists are trying to isolate and classify the basic similarities, or UNIVERSALS, partly by observing closely how children learn a language.

For example, what first words are common to all children? Words like "mama" and "pee-pee," which are pronounced very much alike in many languages, come quite early to children, but such sounds as "r" and "w" and "l" come late (or not at all, in some languages). Thus, a model basic—or universal— phonetic system may be constructed. In grammar, control of irregular-verb forms comes quite late to the child learning his own language, so we may work from a principle of verb regularity in constructing a model basic grammatical system. In syntax, we consider that the visual perception expressed by the structure "I saw two cats" would be similar to all observers, no matter what language they spoke. Likewise, the semantic interpretation would be similar. But in the neural activity, in the thinking process at the deep-structure level, we do not know what order the semantic units are arranged in, or if they appear simultaneously. We assume that this neural activity is universally similar. We have the elements "cat," "I," "two," "see," a plural particle, and a past-tense particle. Their conceptual arrangement may be presented as a vertical column, to suggest that no one element comes before the other at this level:

cat
plural
two
I
see
past tense
} linear surface structure —→ spoken form

We only know that by the time the concept units are spoken in a linear structure—since we cannot project a full, complex thought with only one sound—the syntactical arrangement of the surface structure differs according to the different languages. In English, the word order would be S-V-O (Subject-Verb-Object). In Spanish, it would be the same. In Arabic, however, it would be V-S-O; and in Turkish, S-O-V. The importance of this to the learner of another language is apparent: the realization that the word order of his own language is not the only word order in the world, and that the speakers of two different languages are actually saying the same thing, regardless of word order or the other differences. To some, this is quite a revelation.

Computers and Brains

More and more attention is being given to the similarity between computers and the human brain. Shortly after World

War II, the science of *cybernetics* was introduced, the purpose of this new science being, in part, to find common elements in the functioning of automatic machines and the human brain. This functioning includes memory storage, association, choice, and other mental activities associated with thought and speech-communication. The computer metaphor of human thought and speech has been further extended by a new discipline called *mathematical linguistics*. Table 12-1 shows the data that, we are informed, is "programmed" into our "memory banks" to handle the single item "mother":

TABLE 12-1

Classifications of "Mother"

⟨ + noun⟩	⟨ + human⟩
⟨ + singular⟩	⟨ + kinship⟩
⟨ + count⟩	⟨ − male⟩
⟨ + common⟩	⟨ + older generation⟩
⟨ + concrete⟩	⟨ + same lineality⟩
⟨ + animate⟩	

Just as the computer selects and rejects and organizes at dizzying speeds, so the brain makes the selections and rejections shown in Table 12-1 to form the surface symbol or concept "mother." But just *how* the brain works, what neural processes are involved in manipulating language units and producing speech, we still don't know.

An old question which is still with us is: Can there be thought without language? According to psychologist George A. Miller, thinking is never more precise than the language in which it is expressed. This view would certainly dispute the statement many people make: "I *know* what I want to say; I just can't think of the words." A current view of psychologists and linguists is that concepts are located in the brain system (like the memory bank of a computer), and that they have some sort of electrochemical existence. But what units of speech production are involved in thinking, and how are they directed in speaking? Was primitive, preverbal "thinking" a movielike flashing of images in the mind's eye of early man? One investigator has suggested that brain movements in thinking are connected to the movements of the vocal organs in speaking, that we are really "talking to ourselves" when we think. One area of research in medicine and psychology which is beginning to answer questions about thinking is brain damage. By analyzing what happens when speech fails, specialists are beginning to understand better what happens in the process of normal thinking.

Computers and Language

Through physics and mathematics, the electronic computer has been developed to the point where it can work with language problems, but how far it can go is still a problem for the future. From all that has been discussed in the preceding chapters, we can suppose that the modern view of grammar is of a total set of ordered rules governing all aspects, such as phrase structures and transformations (see pp. 137–40). The selection, as in the computer's memory bank retrieval system, is up to the speaker. But as we have seen, so far we do not have a completely satisfactory theory of grammar. The computer can aid in analyzing various theories of grammar. A set of theoretical rules can be programmed into the computer in ordered sequence—phrase structure rules, transformation rules, and so on. Working at incredibly high speeds, the computer can then generate from these input rules a tremendous number of sentence strings, which may then be checked against a natural language.

Another use of the computer in working with language is "machine translation," or MT. The implications of this are apparent: the Defense Department and the CIA are interested, for military or security reasons, in rapid translations of information coded in foreign languages; such speedy and voluminous translations could also benefit world peace. The breaking of national and cultural barriers could be aided by cross-translations of literary, political, and technical writings, increasing contacts between nations and thereby increasing understanding. And with understanding generally come a reduction of fear and hostility and an increase in sympathy.

However, as a spokesman for the National Science Foundation said some time ago, we do not yet have good, easily used, commonly known methods by which computers can deal with language data. One of the biggest problems that remains is how to handle words with multiple meanings, and ambiguous elements. Take a word like "band"; the computer, resorting to its programmed, or input, dictionary, would have a number of meanings to choose from—or perhaps it would choose them all. Such a problem is illustrated by an excerpt from a machine translation of a 1964 Russian article on space biology:

> Received/obtained by astronauts of the dosage of the radiation at the expense of the primary cosmic emission/radiation and emissions/radiations of the external/outer radiation belt/region/ flange are so/such a small, that can not render/show/give the harmful influence/action/effect on/in/at/to the organism of man. (From *Languages and Machines: Computers in Translation and Linguistics.* Washington, D.C.: National Academy of Sciences, National Research Council, 1966.)

Obviously, further editing by human translators is needed to convert this message into standard, uncomplicated English. So, instead of calling computer-generated translations "machine translations," some scientists now use the term "machine-aided translations" (MAT).

It is sometimes easy to forget that an electronic computer is only a machine and, as such, is limited. It responds to input signals and handles only programmed data. However, it is like a human brain in that it can manipulate symbols and data. And although we know that the computer has limitations, we haven't yet determined what these limitations are. Electronic machines have invented rhymes and composed music, but they are still somewhat baffled by the semantic barrier, as the translated excerpt above indicates. Eventually, perhaps, the machine will "understand" what it is saying, and then another exciting frontier will be opened.

Mathematics has also contributed a new approach to the investigation of meaning. As we saw in the chapter on semantics, ambiguity is always a problem in clear communication, and context is often the key to meaning. The mathematical theory of probability, which deals with the influence of past events on present probabilities, may help to answer some of the questions concerning culture (language) and its effect on the formulation of concepts and on the interpretation of phenomena. In other words, this theory may provide for a closer analysis of the Sapir-Whorf hypothesis of linguistic relativity (see pp. 155–57).

Language—Problems and Hopes

LANGUAGE ENGINEERING is a term used to describe planned efforts to modify a given language. One such effort is that of the French Academy, which we recall was established partly to regulate the French language (see p. 25). While the Academy has compiled and published dictionaries of the French language over the years, it has hardly succeeded in keeping the language "pure." On the other hand, a successful effort in language engineering has been the revival and modification of Hebrew as the national language of Israel. Mainly a written language since biblical times, it was brought up to date and made a uniform spoken language by the "engineering," or "inventing," of new words to fit the times. Another country with an engineered language is Malaya. Because of the diversity of languages and dialects among the population of this relatively new nation, a compromise had to be found between the reality of all this linguistic diversity and the necessity for a unifying national language. While multilingualism is still recognized as beneficial, standard Malay is becoming *the* national language.

A very bleak picture of language engineering is presented in George Orwell's *1984*. *Newspeak*, the government-engineered national language, has been designed specifically for thought control. Docility in the face of harsh government measures is insured because thought is tightly restricted by a limited language. The Sapir-Whorf hypothesis could be carried to no further extreme than this. But we know, from the successful mind-binding of Hitler's propagandists during World War II, when repeated slogans distorted people's thinking, that such an extreme is not entirely impossible.

A problem which we have always had—the need for more effective communication between peoples—has become intensified by the accessibility of travel, the growth of multinational corporations, and the threat of nuclear war. At the international level, this need has been met in part by trade agreements between nations, satellite communication, the "hot line" between heads of different governments, and simultaneous interpreters at the United Nations. At the regional or national level, the need has been met in part by pidginization, as in Hawaii and other parts of the world where commerce has forced a combining of two or more languages into a makeshift working language system which then becomes creolized into a more or less standard dialect (see pp. 53 and 176). The need has also been met in part by adopting a particular language as a lingua franca, or working language. For a thousand years or more, Latin was a lingua franca, mainly among the educated peoples of Europe. In Africa, Hausa serves as a major lingua franca north of the equator, and Swahili south of the equator. On the world scene, English is the primary lingua franca today; whether it will remain so is yet to be seen.

Beginning with the early seventeenth century, philosophers and scientists have reasoned that with a single international language, an INTERLANGUAGE, strife among nations caused by misunderstanding would be reduced considerably, and commercial harmony likewise would benefit everyone. Such a tongue would be an artificial one, with the surface grammar simplified and the emotionalism of a national language avoided. Approximately seven hundred such artificial languages have been tried since the end of the Renaissance. Of these, the one which has met with most success has been ESPERANTO, developed by Dr. L. L. Zamenhof in 1887. Today there are more than five million speakers of Esperanto, and it is taught in six hundred schools internationally. Some airlines and tourist bureaus advertise in Esperanto. And according to Esperantists,

> *La inteligenta persono lernas Esperanton, la lingvo universala, rapide.*

However, a major handicap preventing Esperanto from becoming a truly international language is its obvious basis in Romance languages. For non-Indo-European-language speakers, such as the Chinese, Esperanto would be quite difficult.

Many objections have been raised against an interlanguage. One such objection is linguistic imperialism. This charge is even leveled today against Standard English in the United States by many educators and minority leaders, who claim that the cultural heritage of minority members is submerged or erased by the use of Standard English. On the international scene, the charge would be directed by nationalists against the dominant use of an interlanguage. In spite of such objections, many prominent linguists and statesmen have faith that an interlanguage would positively cure many of the world's ills. But perhaps more than a perfectly designed international language, a new international will is needed, a new spirit of harmony that can rise above nationalistic prejudices and induce the nations of the world to accept an interlanguage. Which comes first?

FOR FURTHER READING

Carroll, John B., *Language and Thought*. Englewood Cliffs, N.J.: Prentice-Hall, 1964.

Delavenay, Emile, *An Introduction to Machine Translation*. New York: Praeger, 1960.

Dillinger, H. E., *Introduction to Esperanto*. Placerville, Calif.: Dillinger's, 1960.

Languages and Machines: Computers in Translation and Linguistics. Washington, D.C.: National Academy of Sciences, National Research Council, 1966.

Miller, George A., *Language and Communication.* New York: McGraw-Hill, 1963.

Orwell, George, *1984.* New York: Harcourt Brace Jovanovich, 1949.

Pei, Mario, *The Story of Language.* New York: New American Library, 1960.

Smith, Alfred G., ed., *Communication and Culture.* New York: Holt, Rinehart and Winston, 1966.

GENERAL BIBLIOGRAPHY

Barber, Charles, *The Story of Speech and Language.* New York: Thomas Y. Crowell, 1965.

Bolinger, Dwight, *Aspects of Language,* 2nd ed. New York: Harcourt Brace Jovanovich, 1975.

Gaeng, Paul A., *Introduction to the Principles of Language.* New York: Harper & Row, 1971.

Hughes, John P., *The Science of Language,* 2nd ed. New York: Random House, 1964.

Laird, Charlton, *The Miracle of Language.* New York: Fawcett World Library, 1972.

Pei, Mario, *The Story of Language.* New York: New American Library, 1960.

Schlauch, Margaret, *The Gift of Language.* New York: Dover, 1955.

GLOSSARY

ABLAUT   Regular alternation of vowels in the roots of some verbs in INDO-EUROPEAN languages, to indicate grammatical changes, such as tense; for example, "sing," "sang," "sung."

ACROPHONIC   Said of a letter of the alphabet whose name begins with the sound of the letter, like "o" ("oh") and "d" ("dee").

AFFIX   A BOUND MORPHEME attached to a base, as in "*pre*payment."

AGGLUTINATIVE   Type of language in which AFFIXES are joined to BASES with little or no change in either the bases or the affixes; examples are Japanese, Hungarian, Turkish.

ALLOMORPH   A variant form of a MORPHEME; for example, the plural ending in "children" and in "trees."

ALLOPHONE   A variant form of a PHONEME, like [t'] in "top," and [t=] in "stop."

ALPHABETIC SYSTEM   A system of writing in which each character represents a specific sound.

ALVEOLAR   A speech-sound formed with the tip of the tongue touching the ALVEOLAR RIDGE, like [t] and [d].

ALVEOLAR RIDGE   The hard ridge of the upper gum.

AMBIGUITY   The property of having two or more distinct meanings, like the sentence "He watched the horse fly."

ANALOGY   The process of constructing a linguistic form by comparison with an apparently similar model; for example, "clockwise," therefore "healthwise," "stylewise," "vacationwise."

ANALYTIC   Type of language in which little or no INFLECTION occurs, and word order largely determines function and meaning; examples are Chinese and, to a great extent, English. Also called *isolating*.

ANALYTIC STAGE   The stage in a child's linguistic development at which he experiments with combinations of language units, testing them on his listeners.

ASPIRATED   A speech-sound that is accompanied by a puff of air, like the initial consonants in "put," "take," "cut."

ASSIMILATION   The process by which a sound changes to more closely resemble a neighboring sound; for example, Middle English *enbrace* became Modern English "embrace."

ASSOCIATIVE FIELD   The various meanings that a single word suggests to the imagination.

AUXILIARY   A verbal element that combines with the main verb to indicate tense, mood, or other aspects of the verb phrase; examples of auxiliaries are "did," "will," "should."

BABBLING STAGE   The early months of a child's linguistic development, during which the sounds he makes have no particular meaning, but signify contentment; he begins to make imitative sounds as well.

BASE   The MORPHEME which carries the main sense of the word, and to which other morphemes may be attached, like "wise" in "unwisely." Also called *root* and, more loosely, *stem*.

BASIC VOCABULARY   Those words in a language that are the least susceptible to change, such as numbers, names of parts of the body and family relationships, and so on.

BIDIALECTALISM   The ability to speak two DIALECTS with equal skill.

BILABIAL   A speech-sound produced by putting the upper and lower lips together, like [b] and [m].

BINARY   Said of a language whose basic structure can be divided into two parts, such as a noun phrase and a verb phrase.

BORROWING   The adopting of words from one language into another.

BOUND MORPHEME   A MORPHEME which does not stand alone, such as "un-" in "unfair."

BOUND SYNTAX   Word order which cannot be changed without changing the meaning of the structure; for example, if the word order of "The man bites the dog" were changed, it would become "The dog bites the man." Compare FREE SYNTAX.

BOW-WOW THEORY   The theory that words developed in imitation of natural sounds, like the "hiss" of a snake and the "gurgle" of a brook. Also called *onomatopoetic* and *echoic*.

CIRCUMLOCUTION   A roundabout, usually wordy, expression.

COGNATE   A word related to a word in another language through a common ancestor language, such as English "father" and Latin *pater*.

COMBINATORY PHONETICS   The area of PHONETICS concerned with JUNCTURE, or the spacing between words, and ASSIMILATION, or the changing of one sound to match another. For example, "It's a nice day" is generally run together as "Itsa nice day."

COMPARATIVE LINGUISTICS   The area of linguistics in which the similarities and differences between two or more languages are analyzed.

COMPARATIVE METHOD   A method of comparing COGNATES from two or more languages to determine the relationship of the languages and to reconstruct the form of the word in the PROTO-LANGUAGE; for example, Sanskrit *asti*, Greek *esti*, and Gothic *ist* are assumed to come from proto-Indo-European **esti*, "is."

COMPETENCE   The ability to understand and produce grammatical sentences in one's native language, even if one has never heard or produced those sentences before. Compare PERFORMANCE.

COMPLEMENTARY DISTRIBUTION   The occurrence in a given language of an ALLOPHONE or an ALLOMORPH in one linguistic ENVIRONMENT and not in another; for example, the plural [iz] occurs in "horses," while [s] occurs in "cats."

CONCORD   Grammatical agreement between two or more words, brought about by INFLECTION, as in English "he was," "they were"; French *le garçon*, *les garçons*.

CONNOTATIVE   Referring to the suggested or inferred associations that, along with the literal meaning, go with a word; for example, "fire" suggests warmth, pain, cooking, terror, desire. Compare DENOTATIVE.

CONSERVATION OF ENERGY   See ECONOMY.

CONSONANT   A speech-sound produced by the partial obstruction or complete stoppage of the air stream somewhere in the speech organs; examples are [b], [g], [s].

CONTENTIVE   A word that has individual meaning, or semantic content, and that belongs in one or more of the FORM CLASSES of noun, verb, adjective, or adverb; examples are "man," "walk," "happy," "slowly." Also called *content word*.

CONTEXT   The particular situation in which a speech event occurs.

CONTINUANT   A speech-sound which can be sounded as long as the breath holds out; the flow of air is not cut off somewhere in the speech apparatus. Continuants include all VOWELS and some CONSONANTS, such as [s], [r], [l], [f]. Compare STOP.

CONTRAST   The distinction made between one word and another based on the fact that the two words differ only in a single meaningful sound; for example, "might," "night"; "quit," "quick." See also MINIMAL PAIR.

CORRESPONDENCE   A similarity between words in related languages; the correspondence may be either the same sound, such as *t* in Sanskrit *trayas*, Greek *treis*, Latin *tres*; or a regularly occurring parallel sound, such as *f* for *p* in German *Fuss*, Latin *pes*; German *Fisch*, Latin *piscis*.

CREOLE   A language which was originally PIDGIN, but has become the first language for succeeding generations of speakers.

CULTURE   The distinguishing beliefs, institutions, and other socially transmitted behavior patterns of a group or a community.

CUNEIFORM   The wedge-shaped characters used in ancient Middle Eastern writing.

CYBERNETICS   The study of control processes in mechanical, electronic, and biological systems, with particular emphasis on the similarities between automatic machines and the human nervous system.

DEEP STRUCTURE   The basic form of a sentence, containing the meaning, which underlies the sentence as it is actually spoken or written (the SURFACE STRUCTURE).

DEMOTIC   The simplified form of ancient Egyptian writing. See also HIERATIC.

DENOTATIVE   Referring to the literal meaning of a word, as opposed to the CONNOTATIVE, or suggested, meanings.

DENTAL   A speech-sound formed with the tip of the tongue touching the upper teeth; for example, [θ], [ð].

DERIVATIONAL AFFIX   An AFFIX which produces FORM CLASS words (nouns, verbs, adjectives, and adverbs) from a common BASE, such as "happiness" and "happily" from "happy." Compare INFLECTIONAL AFFIX.

DESCRIPTIVE GRAMMAR   The systematic listing of the elements of a particular language at a particular time, based on observed characteristics of the language, with no attempt made to evaluate correctness. Compare PRESCRIPTIVE GRAMMAR.

DESCRIPTIVE LINGUISTICS   See SYNCHRONIC LINGUISTICS.

DEVANAGARI   The Sanskrit alphabet, "the divine script of the city."

DIACHRONIC LINGUISTICS   The study of a language as it changes with time; also called *historical linguistics*.

DIALECT   The form of a language spoken in a specific region or by a specific social group, but still understandable to speakers of other forms of the same language; for example, American English and British English, Castilian Spanish and Mexican Spanish. Compare LANGUAGE.

DING-DONG THEORY   The theory that words developed from man's "instinctive" vocal responses to stumuli, just as a bell rings when it is struck.

DIPHTHONG   A VOWEL sound which functions as a single PHONEME, but which is formed by a GLIDE from one vowel to another, like "boy," [bɔɪ]; "buy," [baɪ].

DIRECT METHOD   A language-learning technique in which the student listens to and repeats short phrases spoken by a native speaker.

DIVINE ORIGIN THEORY   The theory that language was bestowed upon man as a divine gift at the moment of his creation.

DRIFT   The minute but constant change that takes place within a language even without the pressures of outside forces, such as war, immigration, or trade.

ECHOIC THEORY   See BOW-WOW THEORY.

ECONOMY The tendency to choose the easier form of a linguistic unit and gradually phase out the more difficult; for example, the initial *h* in Old English *hlaf* was gradually eliminated, yielding Modern English "loaf."

EMPTY MORPHEME Words such as the article "a," the preposition "of," and the conjunction "and," which are structurally necessary to form sentences, but are themselves empty of meaning; also called FUNCTORS. Compare FULL MORPHEME.

ENVIRONMENT The position, within an utterance, of a PHONEME or a MORPHEME, which more or less determines the form the phoneme or morpheme will take. For example, the article "an" appears before a noun beginning with a VOWEL, but "a" appears before a noun beginning with a CONSONANT. Aspirated [p'] appears in the initial position, as in "pit," but unaspirated [p=] follows another consonant, as in "spit" or "help."

EPIGLOTTIS The flap at the root of the tongue which can close off the entrance to the windpipe.

ESPERANTO An artificial, simplified language created in 1887 as an INTERLANGUAGE.

ETYMOLOGY The history and derivation of a word.

FALSE COGNATES Chance similarities in words in nonrelated languages, such as Greek *mati* and Malay *mata*, both meaning "eye."

FAMILY TREE See STAMMBAUM.

FIXED STRESS The characteristic of some languages of having STRESS always on a specific syllable; for example, Hungarian, in which stress is always on the first syllable; or French, in which it is always on the last. Compare FREE STRESS.

FORM CLASS A syntactical classification based on form and grammatical markers; for example, words that follow "the" and take plural endings are classified as Form Class I words.

FORMAL USAGE Grammatical usage appropriate to carefully prepared written or spoken communication—textbooks, lectures, etc.

FREE MORPHEME A MORPHEME which stands alone, such as "fair." Compare BOUND MORPHEME.

FREE STRESS The characteristic of some languages such as English, in which stress may shift from syllable to syllable. Compare FIXED STRESS.

FREE SYNTAX Word order which can be changed without changing the meaning of the structure; for example, if the word order of the Latin "Hominem mordet canis" became "Canis mordet hominem," the meaning would be the same. Compare BOUND SYNTAX.

FRICATIVE   A speech-sound formed by partial closure of the air passages, resulting in friction; for example, [s], [v], [f], [z].

FULL MORPHEME   Words which have individual meaning, or semantic content—nouns, verbs, adjectives, and adverbs. Compare EMPTY MORPHEME.

FUNCTOR   A MORPHEME which does not belong to one of the FORM CLASSES and which has little lexical, or dictionary, meaning, but which functions grammatically, such as articles, prepositions, and conjunctions. Also called *structure words*. See EMPTY MORPHEME.

GENERATIVE-TRANSFORMATIONAL GRAMMAR   A grammar which attempts to explain how an infinite number of simple and complex sentences can be generated and transformed from a limited number of basic structures—usually simple, declarative sentences.

GESTURE THEORY   The theory that words developed from movements of the tongue accompanied by distinctive vocal sounds.

GLIDE   The movement from one VOWEL sound to another, as in the DIPHTHONGS [ɔɪ], [ɑɪ], [eɪ], [ɑʊ].

GLOTTAL STOP   A speech-sound formed by momentarily closing the GLOTTIS, as in "uh-oh!"

GLOTTIS   The space between the VOCAL CORDS at the upper end of the LARYNX.

GLOTTOCHRONOLOGY   The study of the rate of change in language; more specifically, a method, based upon the carbon-14 dating technique, of approximating the date at which one or more languages separated from the parent language. Also called *lexicostatistics*.

GOBBLEDEGOOK   Unclear, often wordy jargon frequently used by bureaucrats and politicians.

GRAMMAR   The system of rules inherent in a language by which sounds (PHONEMES) and forms (MORPHEMES) are arranged to produce sentences. Also, the study of these rules.

GREAT VOWEL SHIFT   A change in the pronunciation of certain English vowels; it took place roughly from the mid-fourteenth to the mid-sixteenth centuries; for example, Middle English *wif* (pronounced "weef") became Modern English "wife."

GRIMM'S LAW   Jakob Grimm's systematic analysis and account of a series of regularly occurring SOUND-SHIFTS between certain Germanic CONSONANTS and the consonants of related words in other INDO-EUROPEAN LANGUAGES; for example, Indo-European *p* became Germanic *f*; *t* became *th*; *k* became *h*.

HIERATIC   The simplified cursive style of Egyptian HIEROGLYPHS. See also DEMOTIC.

HIEROGLYPHS   A system of ancient Egyptian writing, in which pictures of objects were used to represent words. See PICTOGRAPH.

HISTORICAL LINGUISTICS   See DIACHRONIC LINGUISTICS.

HOLOPHRASTIC   The stage in a child's speech development at which he forms one-word sentences, or *holophrases*, like "daddypank" for "daddy spanks."

HOMOPHONE   A word that sounds like another word, but has a different meaning, origin, and, usually, spelling; examples are "sail," "sale"; "beet," "beat." Also called homonym.

HYPERSEMEMICS   In STRATIFICATIONAL GRAMMAR, the layers consisting of experience and meaning.

HYPOPHONEMICS   In STRATIFICATIONAL GRAMMAR, the layer consisting of the physical characteristics of sound.

IDEOGRAPH   See LOGOGRAPH.

IDIOLECT   The unique speech pattern of an individual.

IDIOM   A combination of words, usually a colloquial expression, with a single, distinct meaning; taken separately, the literal meanings of the words do not add up to the meaning of the idiom; examples are "so long," "take it easy," "look me up."

IMMEDIATE CONSTITUENT (IC)   A linguistic analysis based on the principle that a sentence is a two-part construction at several levels. The first two-part breakdown is into subject and predicate; next the subject phrase is divided into its ICs, and then the predicate phrase.

INDO-EUROPEAN LANGUAGE   A member of a language group that includes most of the languages of Eastern and Western Europe and of India; it is the largest language family in the world.

INFIX   An AFFIX that occurs within the BASE of a MORPHEME, like Arabic *kitab*, "book," *kutub*, "books."

INFLECTION   The addition of AFFIXES (in English, usually SUFFIXES) to the BASE of a word to indicate grammatical changes; for example, the addition of plural suffixes to nouns, past-tense suffixes to verbs, comparative suffixes to adjectives.

INFLECTIONAL AFFIX   An AFFIX which indicates grammatical relationships such as number, tense, comparison; for example, "eat," "eat*ing*." Compare DERIVATIONAL AFFIX.

INFORMAL USAGE   Grammatical usage appropriate to casual situations; for example, "It's me," rather than "It is I."

INTERLANGUAGE (INTERLINGUA)   A language which could be taught by all the governments of the world, as the universal language.

INTERNATIONAL PHONETIC ALPHABET (IPA)   A uniform, standardized notational system, based primarily on the Latin alphabet, to represent all the speech-sounds of all the world's languages.

INTONATION PATTERN   The combination of PITCH, STRESS, and JUNCTURE with which an utterance is spoken. See also SUPRASEGMENTAL PHONEME.

ISOGLOSS   A line on a LINGUISTIC ATLAS indicating the area of usage of a particular linguistic item, such as a word or a pronunciation or grammatical characteristic.

ITALIC LANGUAGES   See ROMANCE LANGUAGES.

I-UMLAUT   A sound-change that took place before the seventh century; it was a type of ASSIMILATION, occurring when speakers anticipated an [i] sound in the second syllable of a word, and modified the pronunciation of the vowel in the first syllable accordingly; an example is the Old German plural for "guest," [gɑsti]; the [ɑ], influenced by the final [i], gradually became [ɛ].

JUNCTURE   The breaks or transitions between syllables, words, phrases, and sentences.

JUNGGRAMMATIKER   A group of German scholars who, around 1876, proclaimed a new school of linguistic research based on the principle that phonetic laws admit of no exceptions. Also called *Neogrammarians*.

KERNEL SENTENCE   A simple, active, declarative sentence; most linguists include four to ten or more kernel sentences in the group of basic sentence patterns.

LABIODENTAL   A speech-sound formed with the lower lip and the upper teeth touching; for example, [f], [v].

LANGUAGE   A system of patterned behavior consisting of arbitrary sound-units arranged for the purpose of communication.

LANGUAGE ENGINEERING   The modification of a natural language for a given purpose, like the updating of Hebrew as the national language of Israel, the creation of New Norse in Norway, and the replacement by the Latin script of Persian writing in Turkey and of Chinese characters in Vietnam. Also, the creation of artificial languages, such as Volapuk, Ido, ESPERANTO.

LARYNX   The "voice box" of the throat, identified by the protruding Adam's apple. It contains the VOCAL CORDS and the GLOTTIS.

LATERAL   A speech-sound formed by passing breath along the sides of the tongue, like [l].

LEXICON   The vocabulary of a particular language.

LINGUA FRANCA   A working language used by speakers of different languages. It may be a PIDGIN language or it may be a natural language used by common agreement, such as English.

LINGUISTIC ATLAS   A map of an area, marked off to show the regional distribution of dialectal differences in grammar, pronunciation, and vocabulary. Also called *dialect atlas*.

LINGUISTIC RELATIVITY   The hypothesis that a person's world view is shaped by the structure of the language of his culture, and that therefore the speakers of different languages perceive reality differently. Also called SAPIR-WHORF HYPOTHESIS.

LIQUID   A frictionless, vowellike consonant; for example, [l], [r].

LOCUTION   An utterance; an expression.

LOGOGRAPH   An inscription that symbolizes a word, or the idea behind a word, rather than illustrating an actual object; Chinese written characters are a contemporary example. Also called *ideographs*.

METATHESIS   The transposition of sounds in a word, such as Middle English *bridd*, Modern English "bird."

MIM-MEM TECHNIQUE   The method of language learning in which the student mimics phrases in the target language, and memorizes them through constant repetition.

MINIMAL PAIR   Two utterances differing in only one contrastive PHONEME; for example, "pit"–"pet," "see"–"she," "It's a fool"–"It's a foal." See also CONTRAST.

MODAL AUXILIARY   A FUNCTOR that joins with a verb to indicate futurity, possibility, probability, or necessity; examples are "can," "should," "might," and "will."

MORPHEME   The smallest unit of meaning or grammatical structure. There are two kinds of morphemes; for example, in "feeder," "feed" is a FREE MORPHEME, and "-er" is a BOUND MORPHEME.

MORPHOLOGY   The study of MORPHEMES.

MORPHOPHONEMIC ALTERNATION   Phonological, or sound, variants of MORPHEMES; variants are caused by the phonetic ENVIRONMENT of the morpheme; examples are the plural allomorphs [s ~ z ~ iz].

MULTILINGUALISM   The ability to function with equal facility in two or more languages.

NASAL   A speech-sound formed as air passes through the nose, like [m], [n], [ŋ].

NEOGRAMMARIAN   See JUNGGRAMMATIKER.

NOMINAL   A word which fills the position of noun in a sentence, like "*Swimming* is a great *sport*." Also called *substantive*.

NONSTANDARD   Language usage which does not conform to that generally employed by educated native speakers.

ONOMATOPOETIC   Said of a word formed to imitate, or echo, the sound associated with its REFERENT; examples are "slurp," "zipper," "hiccup."

ONOMATOPOETIC THEORY   See BOW-WOW THEORY.

PALATAL   A speech-sound formed by placing the front of the tongue near or against the hard palate; examples are "y" in "you," "sh" in "she."

PARADIGM   A table showing the complete INFLECTION of a word, such as the declension of a noun or the conjugation of a verb.

PARAPHRASE   An alternate statement of a word, phrase, or sentence, such as "The dog ate the bone"; "The bone was eaten by the dog."

PARSING   The analysis of the words of a sentence according to parts of speech—subject, verb, object, and modifier—and the syntactical arrangement of the words in the sentence. Emphasis is on the analysis of individual words rather than of the sentence as a whole.

PATTERN PRACTICE   A type of language-learning drill in which only one item in a particular pattern is changed at a time; for example, "It's a pen"; "It's a book"; "It's a chair."

PERFORMANCE   A person's actual speech production. Compare COMPETENCE.

PHARYNGEAL   A speech-sound formed in the PHARYNX, by pressing the back of the tongue, low down, near or against the back wall of the throat; an example is Arabic [H].

PHARYNX   A main resonance chamber of the speech apparatus, extending from the nasal cavity to the LARYNX.

PHILOLOGY   Earlier name for DIACHRONIC LINGUISTICS (historical linguistics); primarily the study and classification of written documents, including stone carvings and clay tablets.

PHONE   A separate speech-sound as it is actually produced by the speaker.

PHONEME   A speech-sound as it is interpreted by the hearer; the minimal unit of meaningful or contrastive sound within a particular language.

PHONEMICS   The study of the use of speech-sounds in language.

PHONETICS   The systematic study of the sounds of language and of their production.

PHONOLOGY   A term covering both PHONEMICS and PHONETICS.

PICTOGRAPH   The earliest known writing symbol; a picture of an actual object, used for conveying a message.

PIDGIN   A language that develops from the attempts of peoples of different languages to communicate; the resulting language has a drastically reduced form of the grammatical structure of one of the languages, and some vocabulary from each of the languages; examples are Chinese Pidgin English, Hawaiian Pidgin, Chinook Jargon, African Krio. See also CREOLE.

PITCH The relative highness or lowness of a syllable, depending upon the frequency of vibration of the VOCAL CORDS. In some languages, such as Chinese, pitch can determine meaning; such languages are called *tonal*.

POLYSYNTHETIC Type of language which combines several BOUND MORPHEMES—each one suggesting a grammatical concept, such as subject, verb, or object—into a single unit which becomes, in effect, a "one-word sentence." Examples include Eskimo and American Indian languages.

POOH-POOH THEORY The theory that words developed from emotional expressions, such as "Pooh!" "Pish!" "Bah!"

PREFIX An AFFIX which is attached to the beginning of a BASE; for example, "*anti*toxin," "*un*able."

PRESCRIPTIVE GRAMMAR That grammar which sets forth rules of "correct" usage, often without any logical basis, such as the "shall" "will" rule. Compare DESCRIPTIVE LANGUAGE.

PROPAGANDA The spreading of a particular doctrine or point of view.

PROLIXITY The use of too many words to make a simple statement.

PROTO-INDO-EUROPEAN (PIE) The reconstructed parent language of most of the European languages; also, a speaker of that language. See INDO-EUROPEAN LANGUAGE; RECONSTRUCTION.

PROTO-LANGUAGE The language, recorded or hypothetical, that is the parent of a family of languages; for example, Latin is the parent of the ROMANCE LANGUAGES.

PSYCHOLINGUISTICS The study of the relationship between language and human thought, perception, and behavior.

RECONSTRUCTION The method of determining the form of a word in an unrecorded PROTO-LANGUAGE by comparing COGNATE words from several languages; an example is the following: Maori *tapu*, Hawaiian *kapu*, Samoan *tapu*, and Fijian *tabu* all are assumed to come from proto-Polynesian **tapu*.

REFERENT The thing referred to by a linguistic SYMBOL—for example, in English, the linguistic symbol "cow" refers to the female animal of a particular species.

RESTRICTED SYNTAX See BOUND SYNTAX.

RHETORIC The study of the elements and patterns of language used in effective writing and oratory, particularly persuasive, and the appropriate choice of these elements and patterns.

ROMANCE LANGUAGES   Languages whose parent language was Latin, including French, Spanish, Portuguese, Italian, and Rumanian.

ROOT   See BASE.

RUNIC   The ALPHABETIC system used by early Germanic peoples.

SANDHI   A type of ASSIMILATION in which certain speech-sound losses or changes occur, often when an utterance is spoken rapidly, as in "Can't you?" [kæntʃʊ].

SAPIR-WHORF HYPOTHESIS   The hypothesis that a person's perception of the world and his ways of thinking about it are deeply influenced by the structure of the language he is raised in and speaks. Also called LINGUISTIC RELATIVITY.

SEGMENTAL PHONEME   A consonant or vowel sound indicated by INTERNATIONAL PHONETIC ALPHABET symbols in a sequential, or segmental, arrangement. Compare SUPRASEGMENTAL PHONEME.

SEMANTICS   The study of meaning, and the change in meaning, in language forms.

SEMEMICS   In STRATIFICATIONAL GRAMMAR, the layers containing meaning.

SHIBBOLETH   A word or phrase in one language which is difficult for nonnative speakers to pronounce, and which is therefore used as a password, to identify an enemy.

SOUND-SHIFT   A phonetic change which occurred over several centuries in the early Germanic languages; Proto-Indo-European *p* became Germanic *f*; *t* became *th*; and so on. See also GRIMM'S LAW.

SPECTROGRAPH   A device for representing the sound waves of speech on a graph.

SPEECH   The utterance of articulate, meaningful sound.

SPIRANT   See FRICATIVE.

STAMMBAUM   A "family tree" model used to illustrate the relationship between the INDO-EUROPEAN LANGUAGES and the parent language.

STEM   See BASE.

STOP   A speech-sound formed by complete closure of the air stream; examples are [p], [b], [k], [t], [d]. Compare CONTINUANT.

STRATIFICATIONAL GRAMMAR   A grammar in which linguistic structure is conceived of as a network comparable to the network of the neural connections in the brain. The aim of this grammar is to characterize language as it occurs in the brain.

STRESS   The loudness or softness with which a syllable is uttered. See also FIXED STRESS and FREE STRESS.

STRUCTURAL GRAMMAR   A grammar which attempts to describe a language from strictly observable data, concentrating on the form and function of the elements of utterances first; meaning is considered secondarily. See also DESCRIPTIVE GRAMMAR and FORM CLASS.

STRUCTURALIST SCHOOL   The school of linguistics which developed primarily under the leadership of Leonard Bloomfield from the 1930s on. These linguists concentrated principally on observable and verifiable data in language analysis.

STRUCTURE WORDS   See FUNCTORS.

SUFFIX   An AFFIX which is attached to the end of a BASE; examples are "lega*lly*," "soft*ly*," "happi*ness*."

SUPRASEGMENTAL PHONEME   The speech characteristics of STRESS, PITCH, and JUNCTURE. See also INTONATION PATTERN.

SURFACE STRUCTURE   The grammatical and syntactical arrangement of a sentence as it is actually spoken or written, as opposed to the DEEP STRUCTURE.

SYLLABARY   A list of written characters, each representing a syllable, usually a consonant and a vowel; for example, Japanese *kana:* ka 万 , na 十 .

SYLLABIC SYSTEM   An early system of writing in which characters represented syllables and had phonetic value. It is still used in some languages, including Japanese.

SYMBOL   Any sign, written, spoken, or otherwise represented, which stands for something else. Compare REFERENT.

SYNCHRONIC LINGUISTICS   The study of a language at a particular time; also called *descriptive linguistics*.

SYNTAX   The order in which MORPHEMES are arranged in utterances.

SYNTHETIC   Type of language in which grammatical relationships and meaning are signified by INFLECTION. Latin is a synthetic, or *inflectional*, language.

TAGMEMIC GRAMMAR   A grammar which attempts to combine form and function in basic grammatical units called *tagmemes*. For example, a noun would be considered S : N (Subject-Noun) or O : N (Object-Noun). It also analyzes units larger than the sentence.

TONALITY   See PITCH.

TRANSFORMATION   A rule for changing the DEEP STRUCTURE of a sentence into a different SURFACE STRUCTURE; for example, rewording the KERNEL SENTENCE "John is going home," to "Is John going home?"

TREE DIAGRAM   The schematic representation of a sentence according to GENERATIVE-TRANSFORMATIONAL rules.

UNIVERSALS   Linguistic features common to all languages, such as the fact that all languages have sentences as their fundamental units.

USAGE Language as it is actually used; usage is commonly broken down into three levels: FORMAL, INFORMAL, and NONSTANDARD.

UTTERANCE A spoken expression; a locution.

UVULA The small appendage of the soft palate suspended over the back of the tongue.

UVULAR A speech-sound formed as the UVULA vibrates against the back of the tongue; for example, French and German trilled [R].

VELAR A speech-sound formed as the back of the tongue nears or touches the VELUM; for example [k], [g].

VELUM The soft palate.

VERNER'S LAW Karl Verner's discovery that the apparent irregularities in GRIMM'S LAW could be accounted for by considering the distribution of syllabic STRESS; Verner's law justified the JUNGGRAMMATIKER'S claim of the regularity of sound-change.

VOCAL CORDS Two pairs of bands in the LARYNX which vibrate when air from the lungs passes through them, producing vocal sounds.

VOICED Said of speech-sounds produced by VOCAL CORD vibrations, such as [b], [d], [g].

VOICELESS Said of speech-sounds produced without VOCAL CORD vibrations, such as [p], [t], [k].

VOWEL A speech-sound produced by the tongue and lips, and with practically no obstruction of the air stream—"a," "e," "i," "o," and "u." Compare CONSONANT.

VOWEL HARMONY A characteristic of some languages, in which the vowel of a SUFFIX matches, or harmonizes with, the vowel of the BASE; for example, the Turkish suffix *dir*, "is," changes to harmonize with its base: *kizdir* = "It's a girl"; *kuştur* = "It's a bird."

WAVE THEORY A theory that attempts to explain the wavelike migrations of PROTO-INDO-EUROPEAN speakers outward from their original home, and the consequent language changes.

WORD ORDER See SYNTAX.

YO-HE-HO THEORY The theory that words developed from the strenuous grunts and other explosive vocal sounds of people working together.

INDEX